PRAISE

"As a young doctor, I did not understand why my patients would sometimes say, 'Cancer is the best thing that ever happened to me.' I later learned that confronting cancer can be a turning point that is transformative. This is what Pasha Hogan writes about so powerfully and enchantingly in *Third Time Lucky*, showing us how to identify and eliminate the trivia from our lives and focus on what really matters."

"This book is a joy to read, and I could not put it down. Hogan is that rare author whose voice is so honest and clear that readers fall in love with her and cheer her on as she shares her journey in exquisite detail, warts and all, holding nothing back."

"If you or a loved one have experienced cancer, this book should be at the top of your list. But it is about more than cancer. It is about the inherent creativity and triumphant spirit in everyone, waiting to be freed."

—LARRY DOSSEY, MD, author of *Reinventing Medicine*
and *The Power of Premonitions*

"Pasha Hogan is an inspiration, a consummate storyteller, and a role model for cancer survivors and for *all* women. *Third Time Lucky* is her authentic, beautiful, wrenching, heroic story of creative recovery—a story that inspires me and will inspire you to "live beyond the small version of ourselves."

—PAMELA HALE, author of *Flying Lessons: How to
Be the Pilot of Your Own Life*

"Pasha Hogan has played an integral role with young survivors, empowering them with self-care techniques and strategies to support each other. In *Third Time Lucky: A Creative Recovery*, Pasha dynamically demonstrates the value of connecting young, newly diagnosed women with young survivors of breast cancer to find strength, courage, and hope—so that no young woman faces breast cancer alone, and everyone enjoys access to a *creative recovery*."

—STACY LEWIS, Chief Program Officer
Young Survival Coalition

"Read this book! It will change your life. *Third Time Lucky* is like having an angel by your side, one who blazed the trail you are on, who can reach back and guide you along your journey. Trust me, you will embrace Pasha Hogan as part of your team of angels once you read it."

—JONNY IMERMAN, founder of Imerman Angels

Third Time Lucky

A CREATIVE RECOVERY

PASHA HOGAN

Emerald Flame
Publishing

ISBN-13: 978-0-9885511-0-7 (paperback)
ISBN-13: 978-0-9885511-1-4 (ebook: ePub)
ISBN-13: 978-0-9885511-2-1 (ebook: Kindle / mobi)

Printed in the United States

Cover photograph by iStockphoto©mmac72
and NASA/JPL/California Institute of Technology (PIA04921)
Photo-manipulation by RD Studio
Book design by DesignForBooks.com

Find out more at
www.pashahogan.com

To respect the privacy of others, I have changed the names of
some individuals and altered some identifying details.

For
Shakti

The Divine Feminine and
Creative Spirit that dwells inside us all.

I bow to You.

Re-examine all you have been told....
Dismiss what insults your Soul.

—WALT WHITMAN

Contents

Introduction

I must go on. I can't go on. I'll go on.

—SAMUEL BECKETT

There is an old saying in Ireland: "She's lost the run of herself." I love it. This is often used to describe a situation where someone has strayed off the path of acceptable behavior according to the people around her. This book is for anyone who has lost, or wants to lose, the run of herself.

Cancer was the catalyst for change in my life. I didn't understand this the first time, when I was only twenty-six years old, or even the second time, when I was twenty-nine. If the first two diagnoses were gentle nudges trying to wake me up to my soul's purpose, then the third time was a bulldozer announcing that shocking transformation was on the way! *Third Time Lucky* is my deeply personal story about the events and discoveries I believe were most instrumental in shaping my life and my creative recovery through cancer.

Life doesn't present itself in a perfectly straight line, so neither does my recounting of how my life changed. My story weaves in and out of time and place, each piece contributing to a much larger story that connects us all. We all want to be seen and appreciated. We all want to love and be loved. We all want our lives to matter. That's what cancer taught me. Cancer made my life matter. I want you to understand that your life matters too.

This book isn't just about healing from cancer. It is about life, growth, and the transformation that can take place when we gather the courage first to slow down or even come to a full stop, and next to step into the unexplored horizons of our hearts and souls—without knowing what will happen. If you have ever faced or are facing what feels like a life-or-death situation, be it cancer or some other health issue, a divorce, a career change, or just not knowing what you're "supposed" to be doing with your life, then it is my hope to encourage and inspire you to slow down, pause, and pay attention to the events that have shaped your life—so you can become bigger than them and move toward being your most powerful, loving, and authentic self.

I was motivated to reveal parts of my story in this book to illustrate what can happen when we are willing to stop believing everything we think about ourselves and our lives. Over the past fifteen years, during the course of my recovery and the therapeutic work I have engaged in with individual clients and groups—as a psychotherapist, Reiki Master, and yoga teacher—I have met many incredible people who felt beaten down and trapped by their life circumstances, who felt like life keeps happening *to* them, and who felt powerless to change it. I have also met countless numbers of people who have thought that bad things happened to them as retribution for being a bad person.

For several years, I believed that cancer came to punish me for my past. When unexpected or unwelcome events popped up in my life, often I was quick to judge them as good or bad. But who knows really? We are the ones who give life its meaning by the way we choose to live it. Discovering a more creative way of living was crucial to my own recovery, not only from three bouts of cancer but from deeper wounds and a sense of limitation I wasn't even aware I had been carrying around for most of my life. At times, change was uncomfortable and painful; sometimes it was just plain funny to see how tightly I had been holding on to ideas about the world and myself that I had picked up as a kid. Where does that feeling of never being good enough come from, anyway? Being willing to ask questions and seek the answers empowered me to make lifestyle changes, inside and out, that have made my life better and more fun. I hope this book will empower you to ask the questions that can initiate the changes you want in your own life.

My story isn't over yet, and neither is yours; the healing journey continues. A new story awaits us all. All you have to do is be willing to let go, imagine, dream, and trust. This book is an offering of love and hope, to encourage you to challenge your own thinking and to live into the unknown, beyond your wildest dreams of who you think you are. Believe me, you are much greater than you think.

As luck would have it, the third time saved my life.

CHAPTER

I

i Of The Beholder

The moment when all her resistance to ugliness
vanished was the moment when ugliness became
absolute beauty.

—John O'Donohue

When I opened the mailbox and saw the envelope, it reminded me of the feeling I always had just before I entered the living room on Christmas morning. I knew Santa was coming with gifts, but there was that incessant, secret feeling in the pit of my stomach, and I wondered if he really did see me make that scary face behind my mother's back, or pull my younger sister's hair, or take the dollar from my father's coat pocket. I was afraid that Santa would know that I was really bad and leave me nothing.

I took the envelope from the mailbox and carefully placed it, with both hands, beside me on the passenger seat of my jeep. As much as I wanted to tear the envelope open, a voice inside urged me to wait. Mind you, it wasn't a very caring and compassionate voice, like the one I had been practicing my positive affirmations with in the preceding weeks, oh no—it felt more like a warning voice, like the voice of my Irish grandmother, Lil O'Hara: "Shur, you'll have us all shamed if you open it up here on the street. God knows how you'll react!" It was true. I knew what was inside, and I didn't know or trust how I would react. I decided it would be better to wait to open it until I was home and alone. I couldn't help glancing over at it every few minutes, making sure it was okay each time I hit a pothole or took a sharp bend in the dusty, winding, red road that led to my temporary, new house that I shared with my temporary, new husband, just outside Santa Fe. On the drive, I couldn't help thinking about the bizarre sequence of events that led me to care so much about what was inside the envelope.

Three months previously, I had seen on the notice board of a local chai shop a poster advertising a conference for young women affected by breast cancer. The photographs of smiling faces and colorful scarves lured me to read more. I had never heard of anything like it. Of course, I had heard of conferences for breast cancer but never of one exclusively for women under forty years old. Just before I was first diagnosed, when I was twenty-six, I was told by my doctor that I was too young to get breast cancer. So when I did get breast cancer, I was embarrassed. I was too young, everybody said so. What was wrong with me? Why did I get breast cancer then, if I was too young and had no history of cancer in my family? That was nineteen years ago, when there was no Young Survival Coalition around to say otherwise. That time, all the women in the support groups were old enough to be my mother or grandmother, so I didn't go. I faced it, or rather avoided it, alone.

I read that the conference was being held in Denver, Colorado, the following weekend, and I thought it would be a great idea for me to go and check it out as a kind of field trip to see how my own healing work could fit in.

Denver is about a six-hour drive from Santa Fe, and I had never been to Colorado. Why not? Why wouldn't I go? I could ask a girlfriend to join me and make it into something fun. It never occurred to me for a second that I was one of the people the conference was geared toward: a young woman affected by breast cancer.

My friend, Lisanne, liked the idea of a road trip and agreed to come with me on the condition that she would not have to attend the conference. I didn't even try to convince her, I totally got it. I mean, what woman would want to spend a weekend away surrounded by people close to her own age that all had cancer? No worries, I would go to the conference during the day, she could explore Colorado, and we would meet up in the evening for dinner and drinks. I had it all figured out. It would be fun!

On the first day of the conference, I quickly realized that standing in front of the photographs of the young women on the poster in the chai shop was a very different experience from standing alone among them. It had been such a long time since I even thought of myself as someone who had cancer. I felt totally out of place and wondered what the hell I was doing there. I wasn't having much fun at all. It felt overwhelming to see hundreds of young women who all had breast cancer—many in their early twenties. All of them were wearing different colored leis around their necks. The leis were displayed on a table at the entrance. The idea was that you chose a lei according to how long out you were from your diagnosis. It was a way for people to connect with each other without having to ask all kinds of awkward questions. White was for women newly diagnosed, yellow signified one to five years, green five to ten, and pink was for anyone over ten years out. There was also a purple one for caregivers and friends. Everyone was being honored, wherever they were in their journey. On that first day, I looked at the table covered in leis, thought it was a great idea—for everyone else—and I kept going.

While I was aimlessly roaming around the conference hall by myself, I saw an exhibit table called "i Of The Beholder," and it stopped me in my tracks. I was intrigued by the bold and beautiful photographs on display. I circled the hall a few times and kept coming back to the table, always keeping a safe distance from the brave and courageous women who were writing their names down to participate. I thought the project was a great idea—for someone else—and I kept going.

During the day, I listened to some speakers and attended a few workshops. By the end of the day, I kept feeling my right arm and comparing it to my left, convinced that I had lymphedema after hearing so much about it!

I sat by myself, ate lunch by myself, and spent time writing in my journal during the breaks. What was going on? I didn't get it. I was an open and friendly person. I worked with groups all the time, and people usually liked me. Why was I spending so much time alone?

I sought refuge in my journal that evening, trying to get a clue about my isolation. There it was, written in big, bold letters during one of the breaks, **"I do not want to connect with the fear in the room."** As I sat staring at the sentence, I knew that I did not want to connect with the fear that was rising inside of me. Fear was the familiar feeling I so desperately did not want to acknowledge, the feeling that I had worked so hard to push away over the years. The fear of recurrence.

It was clear that not wanting to feel the fear was keeping me from connecting with myself and the women in the room, putting on a lei, and writing my name down at the table. I realized it was also keeping me apart from the laughter, the fun, and the hope that was also there. I put down my journal and cried myself to sleep—after I asked Lisanne if she thought my right arm was bigger than my left.

The next morning, Lisanne headed off to a tea factory in Boulder, and I made my way toward the conference hall. My first stop was the table with the leis. There were still a few left, and I self-consciously reached for a pink one and put it on. At first it felt weird, but after a little while, the weirdness changed into a quiet joy as I accepted my place in the room and, strangely enough, discovered that I felt more connected with the group just by wearing it.

Not long afterward, a woman wearing a white lei approached me. She wanted to know how I got through it. We stood in the middle of that crowed room and shared parts of our stories, and we laughed and we cried together for almost an hour. I heard about her one-year-old baby and her fears and hopes for herself and for her family. She wanted to live. She wanted to wear a pink lei too one day. I slowly let down my guard and softened into my body and into the room. I knew why I was there.

That first day, when I saw the naked photographs of young breast cancer survivors at the "i Of The Beholder" table, I thought all the women were extremely courageous. The photographs were beautiful, but not something I ever would have considered doing myself. I never would take off my clothes for a nude photograph; it just wasn't me. No way. Gradually, it started to dawn on me that I seemed pretty clear about who I wasn't and what wasn't me. So who was I? What was me? Why wouldn't I take my clothes off for a project like this? What was I afraid of seeing?

On the last day of the conference, when everyone was packing up, my pink lei was my companion as I walked across the hall to put my name down to have my photograph taken. I wanted to be able to stand naked in my vulnerability and in my power. I really wanted to prove to myself that I was okay with how I looked. I wanted to see myself.

On the long drive back to New Mexico, I told Lisanne about writing my name down for "i Of The Beholder." She was curious about my decision, the project, and the photographer. What was it for? Would anyone else see the photos? Who was the photographer? What was she like? I didn't know the answers.

A few weeks later, I received a phone call from Christine Benjamin, thanking me for visiting her table and writing my name down. She was sorry we didn't get a chance to meet in person, and she wanted to introduce herself, her project, and get to know me. In the weeks that had passed, I had imagined having this conversation with Christine, and I decided I wanted to present myself in a cool and confident way. I wanted to let her know that I was really fine with my body, and that I wanted to participate to inspire and empower *other* women.

I forgot all about my plan as soon as we started talking. Christine's voice was calm and thoughtful. She openly shared parts of her story and told me how shocked and scared she was when she found out she had breast cancer, when she was thirty-seven. We talked for a long time on the phone that day, and we discovered that we had a lot more in common than just breast cancer. We were both born in New York, we were both therapists at one time, and we both used our experiences of cancer to change our lives and our lifestyles. Both of us had done a lot of soul searching and decided to put down our private therapy practices for a while to follow the stirrings of our own hearts and to explore our own creativity.

This search led Christine to explore the world with her camera. She discovered a great passion for photography and was intrigued about the interplay that could develop between the image and the person perceiving the image. As a way of dealing with her own feelings about her body after a bilateral mastectomy and reconstruction, she decided to take a series of naked self-portraits. To her surprise, the photographs had a powerful effect. By having a relationship with her image in the photographs, she was able to see herself and her beauty in a different way. She realized that she was on to something, and she started to photograph other young breast cancer survivors. Her "i Of The Beholder" project was born to make a statement about what it is like to be a woman with breast cancer and to help women to see their own beauty in a unique and personal way. For several years, Christine had been traveling around the country, meeting young women who have breast cancer, hearing their stories, and photographing them. Her work also showed the world that the effects of breast cancer go far beyond a pink ribbon. I loved the idea of being part of that message.

Luckily, we also found a lot to laugh about. I admitted that I surprised myself by agreeing to be photographed and told her about initially feeling disconnected from everyone at the conference. I was sorry we did not get a chance to meet too, and by the end of the phone call, I felt I had made a new friend. I was looking forward to meeting her, but neither of us had immediate plans to travel, and she lived in New York. So we left it that we would stay in touch and hope our meeting would take place soon.

A couple of days later, Lisanne called to see if I could go to New York as her assistant stylist on a job for Ralph Lauren; a no-brainer for me. I jumped at the chance. She assured me it was not as glamorous as it sounded and recommended I bring comfortable shoes—a red flag that meant lots of walking, standing on my feet all day, and a new purchase, as I did not even own a pair of "comfortable shoes." I had yet to discover that "assistant stylist" meant I would be steam-ironing sheets, pillowcases, and duvet covers for twelve hours a day. In my naivety, I accepted, as it also meant an opportunity to meet Christine and have my photograph taken.

It was strange meeting Christine for the first time, on a busy New York City sidewalk, knowing she would see me naked that day. A part of me still could not believe that I had flown across the country to take my clothes off for a photograph (and to steam-iron sheets and pillowcases). We agreed to meet at my cousin's apartment where Christine would photograph me. I was surprised by how petite she was and also by how strong she was. The camera bags were heavy, full of lights, tripods, and screens, which would turn the little Upper West Side apartment into a photography studio.

I was excited and nervous to work with Christine. I immediately put the kettle on to make tea, a habit I picked up in Ireland, and we sat across the kitchen table for a couple of hours, picking up where we left off on the phone. She was a great listener and thoughtful in her responses. We got along well, and after the second pot of tea, I felt like opening a bottle of red wine, another habit I picked up in Ireland—but time was getting on, and we had photographs to take while there was still some light streaming in from the gap between the apartment buildings.

I clearly remember telling Christine, at the kitchen table, how comfortable I was with my body, that I loved and accepted it, and I wanted to show myself and the world that there was more to being a woman than having two breasts. That was before I took my clothes off.

All of that appeared to go out the window when all I was wearing was the anxious look on my face. Christine kindly offered some suggestions, from behind her camera, to help me relax, but I felt so self-conscious and exposed that nothing seemed to work. After Christine had been shooting for about ten minutes, she invited me to look at the shots she had taken of me. I imagine she thought that it would be easier for me to relax into the experience, once I could see what she was seeing.

When I looked at the pictures, my attention did not go to the huge scar and empty space where my right breast used to be. My eyes went directly to my remaining breast to see what was wrong with it. I saw a woman I did not recognize. I saw a woman who had a small and unattractive left breast; cellulite on her thighs; arms that were too muscular; and a belly that was not firm. My critical eye only saw a woman who was not *enough*. Where was the woman I had imagined myself to be? The woman who loved her body? At that moment, I realized that I would never be a supermodel. Why the hell was it just occurring to me then? Why did I continue to hold myself up against such an impossibly idealized image of beauty? My attention did not go to my scar, only to what was wrong with the rest of me! It seemed so crazy, yet I was undeniably holding all these super-critical thoughts about my body, and it made me very sad.

I was shocked and devastated by my reaction. I realized that I did not love my body at all. Underneath all the positive words and pretty clothes lurked a harsh critic that was deeply ingrained in me. In that moment, I understood it had been controlling me my whole life. My ego had been running the show. I was in love with the image I had dreamed up of myself, fueled by magazines and glossy advertisements that convinced me I could be beautiful too—if I purchased the right products and did my best to look like someone else. My reaction was so swift and so condemning that it took me by surprise, and all I could do was stand there and cry. I cried for being so hard on myself my whole life. I stood naked in that New York City apartment, sobbing for myself and for every woman who has ever thought she was not enough.

It felt as if my tears released a lifetime of not feeling good enough. Everything appeared so clearly to me that day. In between sobs, I tried to explain to Christine what was happening inside me. I wasn't crying because of how I looked, I was crying because I was so mean to myself, and I couldn't stand it anymore. I had had enough!

Christine was my compassionate witness that day, just like Lisanne was when we drove to Denver and flew to New York. It is important to have a witness when something is being born. And something was, even though I didn't realize it at the time: it was a new relationship with myself.

I don't know how long I stood there sobbing, but eventually I told Christine I wanted to continue. I felt different standing in front of the camera after crying for so long. I felt free. Each click of her camera sounded like an invitation for me to get to know myself. Those tears brought me somewhere that day; I think they brought me closer to home.

When I returned to New Mexico, I called my mom in Ireland to tell her about the photo shoot and what had happened. My mom was always telling me I was enough, and I never believed her. I had no idea how she would respond. Would she think it was crazy to put myself through that, would she think, like my grandmother, that "I'd have us all shamed"? My mother simply said, "If you never did another thing in your life, you would be enough."

No one was home when the envelope and I pulled up to the house. I sat alone on the porch, held the unopened envelope, and whispered to myself, "Promise you won't be mean."

The first thing I saw, when I finally opened the envelope, was a letter from Christine. The opening line was, "I hope you love these photographs as much as I do." The closing line read, "I WANT THE WORLD TO SEE THEM." I took a deep breath and looked at the first photograph; there was no sound. Then the second photograph, the third, fourth, and fifth—still no voice. There was no room for criticism. This time, I saw only a woman; a woman standing still in all her vulnerability and all her power; a woman who was fully alive in both. I sat there with the five photographs scattered around me and wept. I wept for beauty. I also wept with joy, as I fully accepted the woman in the photograph as myself. I saw me.

That was 2006; I was thirty-nine years old, and I saw myself as beautiful for the first time in my life.

2

Burning Boats

My favorite thing is to go where I've never been.

—DIANE ARBUS

I n Irish mythology, the original people of Ireland were the Tuatha Dé Danann (people of the goddess Danu). It is said they came to Ireland because they were banished from heaven for gaining the knowledge of magic. I like to imagine that they are my ancestors.

The Tuatha Dé Danann were mighty and skillful warriors who ruled over Ireland for many centuries. When they were eventually defeated, their victors split the sovereignty of Ireland in half. The Tuatha were granted the half underneath the surface and became known as the rulers of the "otherworld." Now they are called the little people or the fairy folk, who still live underground and come up to the surface to spread their magic wherever they are needed. One legend says that when they landed on the shores of Ireland, they burned their boats, which were full of gold and silver, so there would be no going back to where they came from, in the event they were defeated. Their boats burned for three days and three nights, causing a total eclipse of the sun. When I was young and first heard this story, I couldn't understand why they had to burn their boats. Now I do.

When life presents us with unknown territory, whether we have chosen it or not, life also demands that we move into it. How we move into it is up to us. We can go kicking and screaming, full of resentment and fear, longing to return to before—to what we already know. Alternatively, we can move ahead, still uncertain but with a quiet yet fierce resolve to leave everything we know behind, trusting that what we don't yet know will be revealed to us when we need it most. I didn't always know this. Life showed me. At a young age, I learned that there is no turning back.

The summer I was about to turn fourteen, get my period, start high school, and become interested in boys, my family did something any teenager would dread. We moved from New York, where I was born and had grown up, to a farm in rural Ireland. We didn't arrive on a boat, but even so I knew there was no going back—not until I finished school anyway—and this thought filled me with trepidation.

For as long as I could remember, I knew my family was going to move to Ireland. When I was four years old, my dad took me for a walk in the park. After we got home, Mom asked if I had a good time. "No!" I cried, trying to hold back my tears.

"Why not?" Mom wanted to know.

"Daddy kept singing about Ireland instead of talking to me!" Even as a young child, I felt I was competing with Ireland for my dad's attention.

Both my parents had grown up on farms in different parts of Ireland, and each had separately decided to take the boat across the Atlantic Ocean to New York. My mom was seventeen years old when she left home, and she went only because her older sister didn't want to go by herself. My dad, just a few years older, went in search of his fortune and was determined to return to

Ireland one day with enough money to buy his own farm. They both stopped off at Ellis Island, like millions of Irish immigrants before them, with a few dollars in their pockets and their heads full of dreams, not knowing what lay ahead of them.

They met a few years later, in 1962, at a dancehall in Gaelic Park in the Bronx. By then my mom had fallen in love with New York. My dad never really left Ireland behind, though. He brought his dream with him and carried it everywhere he went. Mom said he told her about it the first night they met and fell in love. He was tall, dark, and handsome, with glistening green eyes; he never drank or smoked and was the best dancer in the place. All good enough reasons to get married, my mother reckoned. Eighteen years and four kids later, they packed up our small apartment, and we flew to Ireland to start our new life.

I had been to Ireland a few times, when I was very young, so I didn't fully remember it. But I did remember some things from the last time I had been there, when I was seven years old. I remembered walking into a small, thatch-roofed cottage and smelling something funny. I learned later that smell was Irish whiskey. The first room we went into was packed with people who all seemed to know my mother. They were hugging her and welcoming her home. Two old men with white hair were sitting in a corner. One had a pipe hanging out of his mouth. Thick, sweet-smelling smoke rose from it. The other man was belting out loud, crazy-sounding music on an accordion, while stomping his foot up and down at great speed. It seemed like a massive party was going on, and I remember feeling slightly nervous but mostly excited.

A lady with wisps of gray hair falling over her kind and wrinkled face bent down and handed me a glass of Coke and a packet of potato chips. A solitary tear fell from her eye into my Coke. I looked up at her and she smiled, so I figured it was okay to take it.

I was delighted with myself, as Mom hardly ever bought us Coke. Glass in hand, I followed my mother into another room, with my five-year-old sister trailing close behind.

Here was a totally different scene. The walls were freshly painted bright white, and a bunch of women sat in lines of chairs packed tightly together. A bed was in the middle of the room. The walls were bare except for a picture of Jesus pointing to his heart that had thorns all around it, and there was a black and white, framed photo of a handsome man in a suit shaking hands with a priest. I found out later that the man in the suit was John F. Kennedy. Everybody had a cup of tea in one hand and a string of rosary beads in the other. They appeared to be moving their lips and whispering something under their breath. I was very proud of myself when I recognized it as a "speedy Gonzales" version of *Hail Mary*, as I had just made my First Holy Communion a few weeks earlier.

My mother went toward the high bed and kneeled down. My sister and I followed her and quickly looked at each other as soon as we got to the bedside, both of our eyes popping out of our heads as our mouths, full of potato chips, flew open. There was an old man lying there. His hands were clasped together over his stomach, and there were dark brown rosary beads wrapped between his fingers. "Mom!" we whispered urgently in unison, tugging at her sweater. "There's a guy in the bed!"

"It's okay," she said quietly. "He's dead." It seemed to be okay with everyone in the room except for my sister and me, because everyone else continued whispering and drinking tea while a huge party was taking place in the kitchen. We both left the house thinking that Irish people were pretty weird.

It was only when I was at my own father's wake, thirty-seven years later, when all the neighbors and farmers came into my parents' house and sat around for two days drinking tea and telling

great stories about my dad, that I truly understood the signifi-
cance of what had been taking place all those years ago: they were
praising and grieving life at the same time.

The year my family moved back to Ireland was 1980; big
hair, big shoulder pads, and big boobs were in. Prior to that, my
only exposure to boys in a social setting was the cafeteria of St.
Barnabas Grammar School in the Bronx, where my eighth-grade
graduation dance was held. I clearly remember the preparations
involved for that one night: shopping with my mother and Aunt
Mary in Cross County for the dress, buying my first pair of
high-heeled shoes, and acquiring "nude" pantyhose that came
in an egg-shaped container. I also had been on my first diet for
several weeks, to look my best for the big occasion, and had
triumphantly lost six pounds. There was so much pressure to
look good for that one night, and it was all anyone ever talked
about in school for months.

To make it worse, the school newspaper had just come out
with the categories that my eighth-grade class voted on. I was
voted the girl with the "nicest hair" and also the "quietest." I
was proud of my long auburn hair but less proud of being voted
"quietest." For me, this equated to being shy, weak, and afraid. I
didn't feel like I was quiet inside, at home, or outside of the class-
room when I was with my cousins or my friends on the block.
At the dance, I was embarrassed and couldn't imagine who would
want to ask me to dance, especially with a label like that attached
to me. But I hid behind the label of "quietest." Although I had
quickly dismissed "nicest hair" as a silly thing to be voted, I was
secretly delighted to have beat Sadie Flynn, who had gorgeous,
long blonde hair. Now that I think of it, I also hid behind my
long, "nicest" hair that night.

To my great surprise and relief, I was asked to dance several
times—always by the smart boys or the ones who were quiet

and nice. They thought I was nice too, another adjective I considered pejorative, until I met boys later on who weren't so nice.

I recently found a photograph of my best friend Donna and me, taken just before we left my family's apartment to go to the dance. Donna looks excited and happy to be dressed up, her heavily made-up eyes beaming, full of anticipation for the night ahead. I am standing beside her, shoulder to shoulder with her, with a blank expression on my face. It is not clear from the photograph whether I was angry or afraid. There was always such a fine line between the two.

When Donna arrived at the apartment door for us to walk to the dance together, I was shocked by how much effort she had put into completely transforming herself. Her glasses were gone and so were her pimples. I had never seen her without her glasses or with makeup. A strange feeling started to rise inside me, a combination of anger and jealousy. My mother and Aunt Mary must have been surprised too, as they couldn't stop telling Donna how great she looked.

Donna proudly explained that her older cousin, Maureen, who worked as a stewardess for Aer Lingus, had made a special trip to her house to put on Donna's makeup and help get her ready for the big night. She looked over at me apologetically and said that Maureen would have helped me too, but she had to go to work. The only makeup I had on was the pale pink lipstick my mother had bought from the Avon lady the week before.

The more my mother told me how good I looked, the angrier I got at her. It was the start of a whole new way of relating with the world: comparing myself to the girl standing beside me or to an image in a magazine. I was always setting myself up to be judged and scrutinized by the most punitive critic in the world: myself.

When my family left New York, I was relieved to leave my labels behind, only to acquire another one when I got to Ireland.

I was quietly proud of my Irish heritage growing up in New York. There was a safety and certainty instilled deep inside me by knowing where I came from. That knowing got burned up when we moved to Ireland. Suddenly, I was no longer what or who I thought I was. The girls in school told me I was a Yank, which was quite confusing, as I had always considered myself to be an Irish girl when I was living in America.

My sister and I had attended Irish dancing school three times a week, attempted to play Irish tunes on the violin, and waved Irish flags while marching down Fifth Avenue during the St. Patrick's Day parade every year. The Clancy Brothers and The Wolfe Tones blasted Irish songs from my parents' record player instead of The Grateful Dead and The Rolling Stones. We were as Irish as you got in New York. That was why I was surprised to find out that I wasn't Irish at all, according to the girls at the Presentation Convent in County Laois—and they had proof.

First of all, they said I talked funny. They loved to imitate my American accent. I found that amusing, as I thought they all sounded hysterical with their flat brogues. Second, I didn't have the right uniform on the first day of school, which consisted of a royal blue, almost ankle-length skirt, a gray shirt with a royal blue tie, a gray V-neck sweater, and brown or black flat shoes with gray knee-high socks. I cried the first day I wore it. I looked at myself in the mirror and was sure my life was over. My only consolation was that none of my friends in New York would see me. I imagined them wearing whatever they wanted to school, or at least pulling up their uniform skirt waistband so the hem was several inches above their knees. Third, it was clear I was a Yank because I didn't have to take Irish language class, much to my classmates' disappointment, as they all hated it. I was a Yank, there was no doubt about it; and being a Yank, the move to Ireland was quite a culture shock.

The day before starting at my new school, Mom suggested I tell everyone that my name was Margaret, and not to mention being called Peggy. Ever since I could remember, my family and friends had always called me Peggy, though teachers, doctors, and other "very important people" did call me Margaret. Margaret was a family name. I had several aunts named Margaret, and it was also my grandmother's name. I am told that when I was about two, my great-aunt Margaret Coolidge's husband Earle, who was American, declared that Margaret was no name for a little girl; according to him it was far too serious. It was decided that, to make it easy to distinguish me from all the other Margarets in the family, I'd be called Peggy. So Margaret was the official name and Peggy was for everything else.

As it was with almost anything my mother suggested to me those pubescent years, I got angry and ignored her advice. I went to school that first day self-conscious of my accent, my appearance, and uncertain of what name to call myself. When I was asked, I told my new classmates my name was Peggy.

One of the major differences between school in the United States and school in the midlands of Ireland, through my fourteen-year-old eyes, was how segregated the girls and the boys were. Unaware of the code of ethics around this rule my first day, I sat in the only available seat on the school bus, which was next to Seamus O'Malley. This innocent and bold move caused quite a commotion on the bus. Everyone turned around and started staring, pointing, whispering, and laughing at me and the red-faced Seamus, who was unfortunate to have had an empty seat beside him. Later, one of the girls on the bus (who turned out to be in my class) pulled me aside and informed me that girls and boys did not sit together. That was the last time I sat next to a boy on the bus on my way to or from school.

The next time I sat next to a boy was a year later, at the local disco. I use the term *disco* here loosely. It was a community hall in a back street of the little town where the Presentation Convent High School and Christian Brothers High School were located. Dances there were put on regularly by the Catholic Youth Association. That meant no alcohol. Sister Maria was also there to ensure that a healthy distance was kept between boys and girls during the slow sets of songs, to keep all of our raging hormones from mingling together. My first kiss took place on that dance floor, after attending for several months. It was sloppy and clumsy and involved his tongue rammed down my throat, which shocked and horrified me as well as all of the girls in my class who witnessed the awkward encounter.

A few years later, I graduated to the local hotel disco scene, where there was a full bar and no Sister Maria. Unlike New York, the legal drinking age in Ireland was eighteen, which I found out really meant sixteen, much to my delight. I was introduced to the Irish confidence booster: alcohol. The boys who were quiet and shy on the bus a couple of years earlier were now loud and amorous after a couple of pints of Guinness. This was the backdrop to my first lessons about alcohol and its transforming effects. I witnessed how much fun people seemed to have after consuming a few drinks, and I wanted to be part of the scene.

Once I had a couple of glasses of Stag, a strong Irish cider, I felt like a different person. I felt attractive, interesting, and out-going—the life and soul of the party. I didn't want to be the Yank anymore or different from the others. I wanted to fit in and drink and party and forget that I felt like a fish out of water.

That's what dating looked like when you lived in rural Ireland in the 1980s: waiting for the hotel disco at the weekend and praying you'd be allowed to go.

In school, we had to attend weekly mass, where I reverently prayed to be allowed to go to the next disco. After mass, we were encouraged to visit the local priest in the dark confessional box, where we would have to kneel down and confess all of our impure thoughts, as there were hardly any opportunities for impure actions. The nuns told us in religion class that to have sex before marriage was a sin. Actually, they also said that the only reason to have sex at all, even when married, is for the sole purpose of having a child. Sex for any other reason was considered a mortal sin, which they said meant you were doomed to burn in hell and no good would ever come of you. Of course, I didn't believe them, but they did a hell of a good job planting seeds of shame, guilt, and doubt in me that grew strong roots. Back then, the disgrace of getting pregnant, to you and your family, was everyone's worst nightmare.

"Well, the Lord save us!" was all my grandmother said when my ten-year-old cousin innocently asked her if she knew what sex was and if she ever had it. In fact, I don't recall ever having had a conversation about sex at home. I learned about periods for the first time by reading a book with my twelve-year-old friends in New York called, comically enough, *Are You There God? It's Me, Margaret.* Now my mother and I talk and laugh about how embarrassed she was to tell me anything about sex. One of seven kids, she grew up in the countryside, where the concept *sex education* was nonexistent. The only expressions she ever heard around the word *sex* were, "Well, the Lord save us!" and "Jesus, Mary, and Joseph!"

In Ireland, my girlfriends and I never talked about having sex or how far we would go. Those subjects were off limits. Sex was the great unknown. Everyone wanted to have it, yet there was so much fear instilled in us about sex to try it. The consequences of "getting a name for yourself" were far too great in our small, rural community. Sex was a secret. Secrets usually lead to isolation, lies, and covering up. Secrets are dangerous. Years later, I would discover just how painful having a secret could be.

Something shifted inside me when we moved to Ireland. I can't say exactly what it was, but it seemed like more of me rose up from the inside to meet the outside world. Maybe this was because I felt disappointed by things not going the way I thought they were supposed to at such a young age, that something woke up inside of me to try and make it better. My expectations of what moving into a big farmhouse would be like differed greatly from the reality. I had wanted things to be magical and happy. When we arrived from the airport at our new home, all I saw was a rundown, old house that no one had lived in for nearly a hundred years. I burst out crying. I didn't see the beautiful homestead my parents had envisioned and which actually came to pass after they spent one full year working on the property, day and night. Seeing my initial reaction, my grandfather shouted out in his heavy, flat brogue, "By *Jaysus,* I heard of young ones crying leaving a place, but not coming into a place!" That was the day I realized that my life would never be the same again. Change is scary. I had to step into the unknown horizon of my heart and soul to keep going, but I didn't realize that was what I was doing.

Though my transition was difficult, there were great things about being a teenager in Ireland too. After a short time in my new school, I took on different labels, like "captain," "editor," and "popular." I was no longer described as "quiet" and somehow managed to blossom into a "fun-loving" and "ambitious" Yank. I was determined to do well in school so I could be the first in my family ever to go to college, and also so I could go back to America as soon as possible. That was my plan.

One of the greatest things for me was being able to ride my ten-speed, bright blue Ross bike for miles and miles throughout the countryside, late into the evenings. I loved my bike so much that we had shipped it over from America when we moved, along with the brand-new furniture my mother bought for our brand-new life. I felt free when I was riding my bike, like anything was possible. I would ride and dream of what life would be like when I left home, lost ten pounds, went to college, got a great job, married a handsome guy, and lived happily ever after. I had it all mapped out in my head. Of course, life seldom turns out the way the way we think it's supposed to; it's usually much bigger than that, with lots of twists, turns, and hills to climb.

For most of my life, I felt I was living in between worlds and identities. Now I can appreciate how moving to Ireland at fourteen shaped me and expanded my idea of myself. I see it more as a source of strength and resiliency that has served me well, making me more adventurous and accepting of different ways of living. As a result of that move, I learned how to adapt to a situation where I had no control and not only survive but thrive—something that I would have to get used to doing for the rest of my life. Instead of carrying my childhood stories as a burden, I have grown to see them as a gift. Sometimes we need to look back and understand where we came from, so we can gather the courage to move forward.

I used to think I was very different from my father. As a child, I couldn't understand his dogged persistence and passion in pursuing his dream of returning to Ireland. Recently I have come to understand it as my legacy. I didn't realize what a mythical figure my father was in my life until he passed away. Shortly before he died, he told me, "You can't beat both sides of the same drum." What he meant was that there comes a point in your life when you have to stand up for what you believe in, make a decision to follow your heart, and keep going. My dreams may be different from my father's dreams, but our longing to live beyond what we already knew and our passion to achieve our heart's desire is the same.

The Tuatha Dé Danann knew they had to burn their boats to move forward into a new life. They trusted that the riches of life lay ahead of them in an unknown landscape, in a life that was longing to reveal itself to them.

One day I too would burn my boats. It wouldn't be so dramatic as to cause an eclipse of the sun, but still, there would be no going back.

CHAPTER

3

No More Running,
No More Hiding

We must be willing to give up the life we planned,
so as to have the life that is waiting for us.

—JOSEPH CAMPBELL

What would you do if someone told you, "You have cancer"? "I would go down to Mexico and stay in one of those places where you just drink juice."

"I would do whatever the doctor told me to do to make it go away—chemo, radiotherapy, surgery—whatever she told me to do."

"I would become a Buddhist, learn to meditate, and develop a positive attitude."

"I would find a medicine man or a shaman and do lots of ceremonies."

"I would freak out."

Most people respond to that question in action mode. They would go somewhere, do something, or change something. I seldom hear, "I would stop." Stop what I am doing, stop running to somewhere else, and embrace this cancer as an incredible opportunity to reevaluate my life, my lifestyle, my story. But sometimes, stopping is what is necessary.

The first two times I was diagnosed with breast cancer, I was too terrified to stop, so I kept on running. I was running so fast, I had no idea what was about to hit me. I received my third cancer diagnosis at age thirty-one, and I didn't see it coming. The third time, I stopped. And it saved my life.

The first time I was diagnosed with breast cancer, I was twenty-six, living in North London with my Scottish boyfriend, and working for a prestigious insurance company in the city. One Saturday afternoon in late August, I indulged myself in a bubble bath, something I hardly ever took the time to do, and was alarmed to feel a pea-sized lump in my right breast. "It's *nothing*," I told myself, yet my fingers kept reaching to touch it.

I only went to the doctor a week later on the insistence of my best friend, so someone else could tell me it was nothing. I remember feeling embarrassed and apologizing for taking up a seat in the busy waiting room. The doctor told me I was too young to get breast cancer. Nevertheless, he decided to do more tests, since my company provided insurance coverage. (I often wonder what would have happened if I'd had no insurance.) A whirlwind of tests followed, appointments all over London, before it was declared another week later that the lump was *something*.

My boyfriend was with me when the surgeon told me it was cancer. All I could do was stare at him in disbelief before I started to cry. I was shocked. There was no history of any type of cancer in my family.

The first person I thought of was my mother. How would I tell my mother? I had no idea what, "you have cancer," meant. Somehow, I found a small voice at the back of my throat and shakily asked, "Does this mean I am going to die?"

The doctor calmly and coldly replied, "Not necessarily."

I received my treatments in a posh private hospital in London. My first night of a three-night stay, the night before the surgery, was surreal. On my arrival, I was handed several menus to select my food choices, which were all served on beautiful china with crystal glasses and fine silverware. It felt more like I was in a fancy hotel than a hospital, except for the fact that I was scheduled to have a lumpectomy and several lymph nodes removed the following morning. My boyfriend came with me and left shortly afterward to catch the Celtic vs. Arsenal soccer match playing on Sky television in the local pub. The whole experience felt like an annoying inconvenience, something to get over as quickly as possible, so we could get back to our regular routines, habits, and lives.

I was uncomfortable with all the attention and visitors, and I remember telling an Irish nurse on duty that I felt guilty for eating several pieces of the chocolate Cadbury Roses someone had left with flowers, afraid that I would put on weight sitting there for days. She looked at me with a pitiful expression, aware that I had no comprehension of how serious the situation was, and told me to have another piece of chocolate, enjoy it, and not to worry about it. In retrospect, I can see it was much easier to be anxious about the effects of the chocolate than the cancer.

Fortunately, my lymph nodes were all clear. Erring on the side of caution, however, my doctor suggested I have six months of chemotherapy followed by six weeks of daily doses of radiotherapy. Since it was discovered at an early stage, only a "mild" dose of chemotherapy was recommended, which meant I wouldn't lose my hair. The word *chemotherapy* scared the hell out of me. I had never known anyone who had chemotherapy, but I had read plenty of magazine articles and heard horror stories about people throwing up for hours and feeling sick all the time. So I put it out of my head completely and never told anyone how terrified I was feeling.

My boyfriend insisted on coming with me for my first chemo treatment, but we fought during the whole tube ride.

When we got there, I was shaking and burst out crying as soon as the kind young nurse asked me how I was doing. I was rattled by how nervous I was feeling and by my outburst of emotion. I had unsuccessfully tried to convince myself it would be fine. Because I was so scared, the nurse asked a woman who was receiving her third chemo treatment to come and talk to me. Her name was Jenny, and she was in her mid-thirties.

Jenny was a lifeline to me that day. She was young, hip, and cheerful, and she didn't look like she had breast cancer. She told me she generally felt a little nausea and fatigue the first few days after treatment, craved spicy Indian food after that, and felt normal for the next two weeks. Then the cycle started again. It wasn't so bad. I wanted to believe her. I had to believe her. So I did believe her.

I didn't lose my hair. I looked great—everyone said so. There was no need to let this get me down. At the hospital, I was encouraged to "go back to normal ASAP," so I did. I went back to work between all of my chemotherapy treatments. I requested the chemotherapy on Fridays, so I could go into work by Monday or Tuesday at the latest each week. I didn't want to make a big deal about my situation. In fact, I was embarrassed to tell people at work I had breast cancer. I was uncomfortable even saying the word *breast* out loud in the first place, and second, I thought breast cancer was something only old ladies got.

When I started daily radiotherapy, I scheduled the treatments for 8:00 a.m., so I could hop on the London underground and get into the city to be at my desk by 9:00 a.m. The radiation being blasted into my body took only a couple of minutes, therefore I reckoned it didn't justify taking the whole day off, and I didn't want my boss to think I was not capable of doing my job. I was grateful to my employers for the insurance coverage and so relieved by their assurance that this "unfortunate incident" would not jeopardize my climb up the corporate ladder.

I made a few changes in the months following my diagnosis. One of the most significant was breaking up with my boyfriend. We hadn't been getting along for months before the diagnosis, and I didn't want to waste any more time in a relationship that wasn't going anywhere. I was excited to be alive! I had no intention of slowing down. I was more determined than ever to live my life to the fullest, which at that time meant doing as much as I could to prove myself at work and partying like there was no tomorrow. "Work hard, play hard" was synonymous with living a full life. It was my personal mantra—before I knew what a mantra was.

Two years later, having put the whole cancer episode behind me, I moved back to Ireland to be closer to my family and friends. I also believed that my London experience in the insurance industry would be welcomed in Dublin and would accelerate my rise to the top. I wanted to make a fresh start by leaving both London and cancer behind. I was twenty-nine years old, and I felt like I had my whole life ahead of me.

After getting over the cancer treatment so quickly, and looking and feeling good, I was full of hope and promise that anything was possible. I thought I was invincible and was confident that I could make a success of my life. Success to me at that time looked like climbing up the corporate ladder, buying designer suits, living in a certain part of town, eating dinners in nice restaurants, enjoying vacations, and looking good—and of course, meeting someone who was successful too. It all sounds quite shallow to me now, but that's how it was.

My London business experience did impress my interviewers, and I was offered a middle management position in the claims department of an Australian reinsurance company. The position wasn't as exciting or glamorous as I would have liked, but I saw it as another step toward my goals. The company paid my relocation expenses from London and promised me plenty of opportunities for international business travel. Though I had never particularly liked working in the insurance industry (or any of my previous jobs), I didn't know anyone else who liked their job either, so I thought of the money, the benefits, and all of the foreign vacations I could afford, said yes to the offer, and just got on with it. It was always too scary to leave the insurance industry, as I didn't know what else I could do in the corporate world. All my business experience was in that area. And there were always the weekends to look forward to.

Shortly after starting my new job in Dublin, it occurred to me: if I got qualified in another area of business, which I might actually find interesting and enjoy, I could come up with another career plan. So I enrolled in a part-time course with the Public Relations Management Institute of Ireland. Classes took place four nights a week. It was an intense schedule and a heavy workload, but I didn't care; I was determined to move out of the insurance industry and into an area that I thought better suited my personality.

After the first semester, I began to realize that the field of public relations wasn't all I thought it was going to be. It felt false to me: creating an image that was attractive on the outside and having no idea what was inside. I was so disappointed, because I had thought public relations was my path to being happy and fulfilled. Unfortunately, I had already paid one year's tuition and didn't want all my time and money to go to waste. I didn't know how to get out of it.

From the moment I arrived in Dublin, my focus was on getting my career on track. It took me six months to finally get around to going to St. Vincent's Hospital for a breast checkup. It seemed like such a waste of time, as I felt great and was back to my old self. When I did, I explained my history to the staff at the clinic and was surprised that they were making such a big deal out of the small swelling where the initial pea-sized lump had been removed. My surgeon in London had assured me that the lump was filled with blood; he'd even put a needle into it to show me the blood and recommended I leave it alone for cosmetic reasons. The Dublin team, however, was not satisfied with this explanation. They insisted a sample be removed for testing immediately. This, however, did not fit in with my plans. I was going to New York City for two weeks over Christmas to party and shop. It would have to wait.

On my return, I checked into St. Vincent's for what I thought was a routine overnight stay for the test. It turned out to be a three-week stay, as there were little cancer cells floating around in that cosmetic swelling. I was convinced that this was a complete fluke and that the surgeon in London did not do his job right the first time. The doctors in Dublin did not confirm my thinking, but they did not discount it either. They were not sure if it was a recurrence or the same tumor.

I was in a state of denial and disbelief. Hearing the first diagnosis, my reaction had been, "What will I tell my mother?" At the second diagnosis, it was, "What will I tell my boss?" I had been with this new company for only six months, and plans were already being made for me to accompany my boss on a business trip across the United States for two weeks in June— there was no way I was going to miss an opportunity like that! I felt insecure about my new position and was afraid of being replaced. To show my boss I was capable of doing my job, I asked him to bring bundles of files into the hospital from the office so I could start preparing for the trip.

I stayed in the hospital, surrounded by files from the office, waiting for the histology report from the tumor for over two weeks. It was during the time of major health cuts in the Irish health service, so I was encouraged not to leave the hospital, otherwise my bed would be taken. Initially, my bed was in the corridor, and then I was moved into a public room with ten other women—a far cry from the treatment I'd received in the private hospital in London. Although I had good health benefits with my new job, private healthcare was denied, as mine was a pre-existing condition.

In the lab, they kept slicing and examining the tumor in an attempt to determine if it was a new cancer or the same one from the first time. Their report would recommend how to proceed. Finally, they concluded that it was not a new cancer, which was good.

When the news was delivered, the head breast nurse sat on my bed and told me I had two choices: I could have a quarter of my breast removed or a full mastectomy. That was it. They did not think chemotherapy was necessary or would be effective, due to the lab results, and I was unable to have radiotherapy again on the same area. Surgery was my only option.

Emotionally, I shut down. There was no way I could have imagined having a full mastectomy at that time. I was horrified at the suggestion of losing my entire breast and was not ready even to deal with thoughts of it. I wanted to do everything I could to save it. Without speaking to anyone or getting a second opinion, I opted for a partial mastectomy. The next day, half of my right breast was removed—they took more than a quarter to be on the safe side—and I was referred to a plastic surgeon. It was confirmed that I would not need any further treatment. The margins were clear; the cancer was all gone.

Again, everyone agreed I was too young: too young to have breast cancer and too young to have half of a breast. For myself, I decided I would put this behind me and get back to my life once again. So I left the hospital with a large bundle of insurance files in one arm and a small prosthesis in the other to balance it all out, totally unaware of how out of balance I really was. I unashamedly used my diagnosis to drop out of the public relations course. The school administration kindly agreed to reimburse the tuition. I knew I needed to come up with a new plan.

As before, the speed at which I got back to my life was impressive. I returned to the office immediately and promised to return to the breast clinic at St. Vincent's every three months. I kept this second bout with cancer very private. I didn't want to draw any more attention to myself for being sick. Everything was okay now. I went on the business trip four months later. It was a success. I had proved my worthiness, and more trips followed.

In the meantime, I jumped into the Dublin social scene, which involved drinks and sometimes dancing after work and dinner parties at the weekends. I kept busy. A few months after my stay in the hospital, I met an eligible young businessman on a flight back from the States, and we became friends—kind of. We were the kind of friends who found each other attractive, flirted, confided in each other about our discontentment with careers, relationships, politics, etc., but neither of us ever made a move. I liked him and imagined he liked me too, until I was at a dinner party at his house, and he disappeared upstairs with another guest, who was also his "kind of" friend.

That was one of a number of friendships with men—or rather, flirtations—that never went anywhere. I wondered what was wrong with me. I hadn't been in a relationship for nearly three years. I was certainly embarrassed about my two stints with breast cancer and never talked about them with men and hardly ever with my girlfriends. I was also uncomfortable and embarrassed by my body. I think I always was, but my discomfort was brought to light by the second surgery.

All my doctors, nurses, friends, and even my mom encouraged me to have breast reconstruction surgery. Everyone agreed that it would be a shame to have to go around for the rest of my life with only half of a breast. Everyone had my best interests at heart. After all, I was a reasonably attractive and single woman with hopes of meeting my knight in shining armor. Why be at a disadvantage? It was hard enough to meet a guy as it was. Why make it harder for myself? However, I waited for a year before I had a consultation with a plastic surgeon.

I was reluctant to have breast reconstruction. Over the years, I'd read hundreds of claims files alleging that leaking silicone breast implants had caused women serious health problems, such as lupus and other degenerative diseases. I'd seen disfiguring pictures and read devastating stories, which often had me in tears at my desk. Personally, I was convinced there was some truth to all the allegations, and I didn't want to invite trouble by putting silicone implants in my chest.

The plastic surgeon I was referred to in Dublin dismissed my concerns as "rubbish" and told me there was no proof. He used silicone implants all the time in his practice and claimed he had seen only good results. As far as he was concerned, I was being ridiculous, and he let me know it in a condescending manner. He also told me it was harder to reconstruct half a breast, and he'd be able to guarantee better cosmetic results if my entire breast had been removed. Unfortunately, this man was the only plastic surgeon available to me in the hospital, so I had to deal with him despite my dislike of his demeanor.

The other option the surgeon gave me was saline (salt water) implants, which he discouraged, as he said they would not feel or look as natural as silicone implants. The surgery would be more extensive: balloon-type expanders would have to be inserted in the tissue around my breasts and then gradually "pumped up" over a few months, followed by another surgery. It was a lengthy process. Although I did not like the idea of visiting the surgeon so often and having so many surgeries, I opted for the saline over the silicone. He also advised me to have a saline implant in my left healthy breast, so I would look better—I'd appear more balanced.

As much as I did not like that particular surgeon, I understood he had an excellent reputation and decided to follow his advice. I also felt the pressure to "look balanced." Throughout the entire experience, I felt like a piece of meat. There is no other way to put it. I was uncomfortable with the whole process. My intuition whispered not to do it, but I didn't listen.

When I woke up from the final reconstructive surgery, I was in excruciating pain. I have a high threshold for pain and don't like to complain, but I'd never experienced anything like that before. I complained, cried, and begged them to take the pain away. My surgeon sent me home with some painkillers and told me to call his secretary to make a follow-up appointment. He assured me the pain would ease in time. It did not. I was in pain every day for six months.

I had left the public relations course because its focus was all on image without a lot of concern for substance. At the time, I reserved that judgment for the course. I couldn't see yet that I was suffering from the same misplaced focus. Over the next few months, that started to change for me; something was shifting from the inside. I was discontented with my personal life and professional life, and they both seemed so separate and far apart from each other. Something was missing. I started to question my personal image. I started to question why I was putting so much energy into my work when I didn't even like it. I began to wonder what it would be like to work in a field I actually enjoyed. I started to reevaluate what being a successful person meant and why getting closer to my idea of success had never made me happy.

I confided my dissatisfaction to a nurse at the breast clinic during one of my routine checkups, and it turned out she was also a psychotherapist. Her name was Freda. We made a counseling contract to see each other once a week for six weeks. I had never considered therapy as an option before, but after six weeks, I was hooked on it and continued to see Freda on a weekly basis to talk, as well as at the breast clinic every three months.

Therapy was a whole new experience. I wasn't used to sitting opposite someone and talking about myself—unless I was in a pub, of course. Historically, the pub and the confession box were Ireland's answer to therapy. In the 1980s and '90s, therapy was considered "very American" by most Irish people, who were either suspicious of it or made fun of it. So I initially kept my weekly excursions to see Freda to myself. Week after week, I showed up in her office in my suit on my way home from work. I talked about how I felt like a phony at work, how I wanted a new career, and how I didn't want to let breast cancer identify me or become a big deal in my life. I needed a new plan, and I wanted her to help me.

Entering into the therapeutic process was a major turning point. It enabled me to identify a number of core beliefs I held around being powerful, feminine, and successful, and how those beliefs were no longer serving me. I started to see how hard I was on myself and how easily I let my punitive inner critic run the show. I became aware of the fast pace I was keeping. I slowly emerged from the corner I'd backed myself into around work and the belief that there was no way out. Therapy sessions began to feel like public relations from the inside out. I loved going inside and exploring for the answers to my questions. I felt passionate in my search for living an authentic life and wanted to share my passion with others. That was it! A new plan emerged one year later: I would train to become a therapist.

I decided to apply for part-time enrollment in a professional psychotherapy and counseling course. It would take place on weekends over three years, so I could do it and still work full time.

I filled out my application form, wrote my personal statement, attended my interview, and waited.

Three weeks later—which seemed like an eternity—an official, cream-colored envelope arrived in the mail. I held the unopened envelope in my hand, closed my eyes, and prayed. This could be my passport out of insurance. I opened the envelope with trepidation, afraid I might have been rejected. The letter read: "This is to inform you that you have been accepted on the part-time Psychotherapy and Counseling Training Course commencing September 1997." Yes! I was overjoyed. I couldn't wait to go the clinic the next day and tell my therapist.

I rushed over to my stereo and pushed track number three. The lyrics of R.E.M. filled the room as I jumped up and down with excitement to the song, "It's the End of the World as We Know It (And I Feel Fine)."

The previous Friday had been my regular three-month visit to the breast clinic. After going regularly for two years since the second diagnosis, I had a good relationship with the whole team. It seemed more of a social visit to me, at that stage, than a health visit. The worst part was the long delay in the waiting room; I often had to pass up to four hours to be seen. Imagine being in a crowded room where every woman sitting there either had breast cancer or was wondering if she had breast cancer. The tension was palpable. During that routine visit, my doctor decided to take a little sample from a fatty tissue he felt on my right breast. He would send it off to the lab, and then I would have to come back the following Friday for the results. Nothing to worry about. He told me he was just being hyper vigilant, given my history. The following week, I gave my name at the reception desk and bounced into the waiting room with the cream-colored letter in my bag. I settled into my plastic brown chair and picked up *Marie Claire* magazine to prepare myself for the long wait. I was only halfway through my first article when I felt a tap on my shoulder. I looked up and was surprised to see Freda standing there. She had her white lab coat on and beckoned me to follow her down the corridor leading to the consulting rooms. I felt a huge urgency to let her know my good news before we reached the end of the corridor. Wanting her to see the letter, I reached for it in my bag and blurted out that I had been accepted into the course. Freda gave me a big smile. But I couldn't help noticing that she didn't look very happy.

I entered the little cubicle and decided not to put on the blue paper gown that lay neatly folded on the examining table. Moments later, my doctor entered the room with my thick file in his arm, followed by the head breast nurse and my therapist. Shit! I thought. Why are all these people here? My stomach started to turn as he opened his mouth, and before he could say anything, I also told him I'd gotten accepted into the psychotherapy training course. I was hoping that, once everyone heard my good news, there would be no room for any bad news.

No pleasantries were exchanged. "It's cancer. I am sorry."

He said it so fast. I didn't cry—there would be plenty of time for that later. I just looked at the three of them in disbelief. How could he tell me that when I *finally* had a new plan? I let out a sigh that felt like it had been trapped forever. "What does that mean now?" I asked, digging my nails into my sweaty fists, so afraid of what he would say next. Would I die this time?

He said it meant I had to have surgery right away to remove my right breast completely. There was no room for protest. They would give me the strongest and meanest chemotherapy they could this time—no more pretending it was okay. This cancer was obviously aggressive, and that's how they were going to treat it. They would call me on Monday and schedule more tests to determine if it had spread. The consultation was over. This time, my question changed from, "How quickly can I get back to normal?" to "How long do I have to live?"

When I left the hospital, I went directly back to my apartment and pushed track number three on the stereo again. "It's the End of the World as We Know It (And I Feel Fine)" blared out from the speakers, filling the room, but I didn't jump around as I normally did when I heard that song. Instead, I sat on the floor, still in my suit, and looked down at my perfectly balanced breasts. The world as I knew it ended that day, and strangely, I did feel fine. I silently promised myself that there would be no going back to normal. I figured normal wasn't so great anyway, since it had brought me to a third diagnosis of cancer.

I knew life had to be different. There would be no more warnings. I had to pay attention and start listening to my body, my dreams, and my soul. However, I had no idea how to do that. So I moved home to the farm in the middle of nowhere that I'd hated moving to when I was a teenager. I couldn't imagine what it would be like living there with my parents at thirty-one.

When I told everyone at home what I was about to undergo, the first thing they wanted to know was, would I lose my hair? Ever since I was a kid, I'd always had long auburn hair. I only cut my hair short once, just before my prom (in reaction to being dumped by my first boyfriend). I clearly remember hearing my best friend's boyfriend shout across the disco floor in a very heavy Irish accent, "You destroyed *yerself!*" My memories of having short hair offered no consolation as I got ready to have no hair at all. Though I did not like the idea of losing my hair, I was far more concerned with losing my breast.

A few days before the surgery, I was sitting at the kitchen table in my pajamas reading the back page of *The Irish Times*, and I saw an advertisement for a "holistic fair" taking place in Dublin, about sixty miles away. I had never been to a fair such as this, and as soon as I saw the ad, I knew I had to go. I don't know how I knew, I just did. Two hours later, I was walking around the Royal Dublin Society Hall in a daze. Every crystal healer, tarot reader, reflexologist, psychic, meditator, and vegan in the country seemed to be there. The place was packed. I was shocked to see thousands of people milling around, all in search of some healing. I felt so alone, despite being surrounded by people everywhere I turned.

It felt strange to be there, strange to be walking around in circles—no one knowing that I was carrying cancer in my body. No one knowing that, in a few days, I would have only one breast, and in a few weeks, no hair.

I started watching people and wondered what everyone was searching for. I would look at a complete stranger and think she was the luckiest person in the world. Lucky not to have cancer.

There was one stall that really stood out. The sign read: "Reiki." I'd never heard of Reiki before, but that didn't surprise me, as I hadn't heard of most of the things being offered at the fair. A woman was doing ten-minute demonstrations for a suggested donation of five pounds. Reiki turned out to be some kind of energy work. Usually, that was enough to get my inner skeptic jumping up and down and me exiting stage left as swiftly as possible, but that day was different. I hung around for a demonstration along with a few other people.

It appeared that all you had to do was lie on a massage table while the woman placed her hands over your body. A white muslin curtain surrounded the table. Soft music was playing and incense was burning. It looked relaxing, and I was exhausted from all the driving and battling the crowds. After a while, I got fed up with waiting and did another lap around the hall. Nothing else interested me. It was obvious to me that I was just filling time until I could get back to the Reiki stall. The same feeling that made me get up from the kitchen table kept luring me back.

I was beginning to feel embarrassed. I felt like a stalker. Every time I went over, the gray-haired lady with the English accent at the adjoining booth told me to come back in five or ten minutes. I must have gone back four times, which was totally unlike me, as I never liked to appear needy. Finally, the English woman invited me to sit down in her stall and wait. Her name was Hazel. She had long, wild gray hair, wore a multicolored, loose-fitting dress, and had a big moonstone ring on her middle finger and lots of bracelets jangling along her arm. I'd never met anyone like her. There was no sign over her stall, so I had no idea what kind of thing she was offering.

I had been sitting there quietly and anxiously for a few minutes, wondering what would happen on the other side of the white muslin curtain when it was my turn, when Hazel held out a bowl of colored paper and invited me to take one.

"What's this?" I asked suspiciously.

"A gift for you," she replied. "It doesn't cost anything. Please just take one."

I reached into the bowl and took a red piece of paper. I unfolded it and read: "Why are you here?" That was it. I just sat there staring at it.

To my great surprise, within a few seconds I started breathing faster. I could feel beads of sweat surfacing on my forehead. I couldn't speak. All I could do was sit there and stare at those words. "Why are you here?" Tears slowly ran down my face, staining the little red piece of paper on my lap. A strange tingling sensation started spreading all over my body. I had never experienced anything like that, and it was starting to scare me. I heard the words, "I am here for a reason," come out of my mouth, and I was startled by the sound of my own voice.

I have no idea how long I sat on that low wooden chair before Hazel helped me lie down on the Reiki table next door. Time just seemed to stop. I could hear American Indian drumming music in the background. I felt safe, even though I had no idea what was happening. My face had the sensation of pins and needles all over it, and it felt like it was slowly being twisted. It was difficult to get out the words to articulate the strange sensation. It seemed I had no control over my facial muscles to speak. I desperately wanted to communicate the strange feeling. I had to let someone else know what was going on.

Out of nowhere another woman's voice said, "It's all the masks starting to peel off, don't worry." It was the woman giving the Reiki demonstrations.

The soft sounds of the Indian drumming accompanied the first few masks on their way off. That phrase helped me to understand all that was happening and all that was about to happen. I understood: it was time for all the masks to come off.

When I got home from Dublin later that night (it turned out I was on the Reiki table for over an hour), I was so excited to share my experience with my mom, dad, sister-in-law, and brother. As soon as I started talking about it, I could see their eyes darting to meet each other's, and I knew they thought I'd either imagined the whole thing or was losing it under the pressure. I didn't care. I knew I experienced something amazing, even if I didn't understand it.

The Reiki lady's name was Karen. She also lived in the middle of nowhere, about a thirty-minute drive from my parents' house. I was astonished to find out that someone like her lived near my parents in the Irish midlands. She had given me her number before I left the fair, and we met weekly for the next six months. She helped through all of my chemo and drove to my parents' house to give me Reiki treatments when I was too wiped out to go to her. I discovered that *Reiki* is a Japanese word that means "life force energy," and it is used for healing all over the world.

My relationship with Karen and Reiki helped change my relationship with myself and my life, and it altered how I saw the world. That day, I realized the world was a much bigger place than I had ever dared to imagine. If that experience was possible, what else could be?

The night before my mastectomy, the nurse on duty looked familiar, and we started talking. We discovered we frequented the same pubs in town and were around the same age. She told me it was her last shift in that hospital. She was moving to Australia in a few days to start a new life Down Under. I was excited for her. My cousin Marie also was a nurse, and she'd spent a year in Sydney and loved it.

We were having a good conversation, joking around about adventures, pubs, and new beginnings, when the nurse suddenly stopped talking. She looked at me with tears in her eyes and said, "You are too young to lose your breast. I am so sorry you have to go through this." I knew she meant it—and then it hit me: the next day I would have only one breast. I would miss it. I'd never thought about missing it before, I'd only thought about getting the cancer out of my body. I burst into tears and immediately apologized for crying. They were quiet tears, but I tried to choke them back, so I wouldn't upset the elderly patients on either side of me.

The young nurse sat on the edge of my bed, hugged me with fierce compassion, and encouraged me to cry. "You need to grieve your loss," she said. I cried in her arms until no more tears were left and then drifted off to sleep. When I woke up the next morning, the nurse had already left. Her shift was over. And a new life awaited both of us.

On the way to the operating room, I asked the surgeon to take out the saline implant in my remaining left breast, when he took off my entire right breast. My body had been through enough. The implants had been nothing but a source of pain and discomfort for the six months they were there, and I wanted them gone.

A few months after my mastectomy, I was standing in my bedroom looking in the mirror, the same mirror I had stood in front of for hours as a teenager, squeezing my body into tight jeans, stuffing toilet paper into my bra, experimenting with makeup, and trying to straighten my 1980s big hair, all in an effort to look cool. My efforts never quite worked to my satisfaction. This time, I saw a stranger looking back at me. She had no hair, hardly any eyebrows or eyelashes, and dark circles underneath her eyes. Her face was swollen and fat from all the drugs and steroids being pumped into her body every three weeks. But it was the eyes I recognized first. They were hazel with dark speckles, and they looked lost and sad. I looked at this stranger, and her eyes cried out to me. Don't go! they pleaded. If you leave me now, I will have no one. I need you to stay.

They say the eyes are the gateway to the soul, and that day I believed it. I looked back at this stranger, who had loved me all of my life. I hadn't even known it. I felt so much compassion and love for her.

Just at that moment, my mom walked in with some folded laundry. That was usually my cue to pull it together and be cheerful—for her sake, I thought. But I couldn't do it that day. My eyes had melted all my defenses. I looked straight at her and said, "Mom, I'm scared."

To my surprise, her blue eyes filled with tears and she replied, "I'm scared too."

The exchange was so simple, so honest, and so real that we fell into each other's arms and cried like we had never cried before. In fact, I'd never heard my mother cry or felt her body shake in my arms as she wept. We fell on the bed and then started laughing when we fell off the bed! It was such a relief, for both of us to cry, to fall, and to laugh. Our relationship changed forever that day, and so did my relationship with my life.

It was the start of learning how to listen to my body, my dreams, my soul. I consciously decided to stop that day. Stopping would make all the difference. No more running. No more hiding. I had resisted stopping my whole life. It certainly was the end of the world as I knew it—and the beginning of a whole new life for me.

Stopping allowed me to accept and feel whatever I was experiencing instead of explaining it away with my rational brain or holding the tension of it in my body until I thought I could deal with it later. My rational brain had told me I wouldn't get cancer again. My rational voice had told me Reiki was for eccentric and New Agey people. Now I stopped giving all of my power over to the rational. "Being before doing" became my new mantra, and this time, I did know what a mantra was.

It takes courage to stop. Still, I don't always want to. But I have learned that life is a series of stops and starts. When I forget this now, I look at myself in the mirror, I see my scars, and I remember how stopping saved my life—and I am grateful.

A few years ago, a friend told me about a dream she'd had. In the dream my name was Lucky Hogan. She thought it was funny and strange, as she would hardly call me lucky, given my history with cancer. I loved it! I am lucky. Lucky to be able to let go of my plans and live life fully into the unknown. Lucky to have to learn all over again how to live.

CHAPTER

4

Becoming Bigger
Than the Story

Remembering is not the negative of forgetting.
Remembering is a form of forgetting.

—MILAN KUNDERA

M y philosophy on life since I was ten years old was: "One big thing happens to everybody." That was my way of making sense of the senseless things that happen to people. When I was a kid, I thought no big thing had ever happened to me. I never got sick, except for tonsillitis twice a year, every May and October, like clockwork. My mother refused to let my tonsils be taken out, much to my disappointment, as I heard the other kids in school talking about all the ice cream they got to eat afterward. I never even got the chicken pox or measles until I was in college, which was very embarrassing. Never broke an arm or ankle. Nothing.

My parents were together. Mom stayed at home and had dinner waiting for us every night. In contrast, my friend's father drowned one year while they were on vacation, and my Aunt Kathleen died, leaving behind my nine-year-old and two-year-old cousins. Most kids I knew had spent at least a night in a hospital or their parents were separated. I thought I had a pretty happy and uneventful childhood—at least until I started therapy.

When I was diagnosed with breast cancer, my "one big thing" theory was blown apart. I thought my one big thing had happened before any of the cancer. I wanted to forget that night and that summer. I coped by forgetting what I couldn't handle. I couldn't handle the car accident.

Nine years after my one big thing, I talked about it openly for the first time with Freda in therapy, just prior to my third diagnosis and encounter with Reiki. I didn't know how to talk about it before then.

The day before the car accident, I broke up with Shane, my first and only boyfriend, over the phone. It was 1987, and I was on Easter break during my third year of college. Shane had moved to London for work a few months earlier and was supposed to come home to celebrate his twenty-first birthday. I'd been looking forward to his visit for weeks and had "borrowed" my college roommate Ellen's prized pink skirt for the big occasion. She had a closet full of fabulous clothes. She didn't know I borrowed her skirt, but I figured I would be able to put it back before she ever knew—no harm done. When Shane called to tell me at the last minute that he couldn't make it home, I flipped. I told him I was fed up with our long-distance relationship and I wanted it to be over once and for all.

I already had made plans to go to New York for the summer with a friend from college. I wanted to be free and boyfriend-less, have some fun, make some money, and return to Ireland in September to finish my final year of college. I thought I'd made it clear to Shane from the start: after college, I was going to return with my business degree to New York, permanently, to make a success of my life on Wall Street. We had no future together. There was no point in dragging it on any longer.

Shane freaked out and flew home the next day. He called me from the airport to tell me that he would see me in a few hours. I told him to forget it, that he was wasting his time and money. He insisted. I was furious but secretly flattered, which did nothing to help me stick to my word. There was so much pressure to go out that night from him and his sisters, who started phoning me as soon as they heard that I had broken it off. I was weak. I didn't know how to say no and didn't want everyone to think I was a bitch. So I reluctantly arranged to meet them all in the local village pub. I told Shane I would go out with him one last time, since he'd traveled from London. I insisted that it was still over, my meeting him meant nothing. He didn't believe me.

The arrangements were made. There was a popular band from Dublin playing in the small country town ten miles away; his two brothers and three sisters would all be there with their girlfriends and boyfriends. Everyone—but me—was looking forward to a great night out. A few cars were going to the venue, and I caught a ride with Pete, Shane's younger brother, who was nineteen. He made the big sacrifice of driving and not drinking that night so we could all go. Pete was a good friend of mine and was well accustomed to the ups and downs of the dramatic young love between his brother and me.

I spent most of the night in a bad mood, doing my best to get lost in the crowd in an attempt to lose Shane. Finally, the last song was played, the lights were turned up, and it was time to go home. Six of us packed into Pete's little silver Ford Fiesta. It was so cramped in the backseat that I had to sit on Shane's lap with my head reaching forward between the two front seats. Pete was aware of our breaking up and my bad mood. He kindly asked me if I wanted to be dropped off first. "Yes! Please just bring me home!" That was the last thing that was said before I was blinded by an incredible light. I gasped and closed my eyes.

The lights I saw were the headlights of a speeding car headed straight toward us. It was on the wrong side of the road, a drunk driver behind the wheel. I opened my eyes again, sometime later, and wished I hadn't. It was pitch black and hard to see at first. I didn't know where I was or what had happened. I thought I was alone in a very small, dark space. I felt a great pressure across my right foot. I looked up and saw Pete. He was thrown back onto the seat with the steering wheel crushing his chest. His mouth was open, but there was no sound.

Then I saw Shane to the left of me; his eyes were closed, and he was completely still. He was covered in glass and blood. I started screaming at the top of my lungs: "Get me out! Get me out! Get me out!" I was desperate to get away from the darkness and the silence that surrounded me. But I couldn't move; there was no feeling in my legs. Was I paralyzed? I looked down at my lap, which was completely covered in blood, and instantly thought, Oh my God, Ellen's skirt. She'll kill me!

I started to panic over the skirt, which was unrecognizable, drenched in blood. Then I heard a young woman's voice, one I didn't know. It was soft and soothing, "It's okay. They're going to get you out soon." I started crying. She reached in and held my hand. She listened as I sobbed and pleaded to get out. She explained that they were waiting for the firemen to come to cut me out of the wreck. She told me the others were okay and had been able to crawl out a window. Later I was told the car was a total write off.

After a few minutes, I noticed that my tongue was hanging outside the left side of my face; there was no skin to keep it inside. It was all too much. I couldn't take it in and I couldn't bear to look at Pete's and Shane's bodies. I focused on the blood-drenched skirt instead. I told the young woman about Ellen's skirt and how much trouble I'd be in when she found out I took it. I went on and on about the skirt until the firemen came. Then I probably told them too.

The silence quickly turned into chaos. There were sirens and shouting, and I could hear the grief-stricken cries of Shane's sisters. It turned out they were following us in a car not far behind and drove upon the horrific scene. I am not sure how long I was trapped inside the car, it may have only been fifteen minutes, but it seemed like an eternity.

Once they got me out, I was placed on my back in the middle of a field to wait for the ambulance. I saw Shane's youngest brother Joe, who was also in the car, and two other girls I didn't know, who had asked us for a lift home. They were injured but conscious. Everyone was crying. From the corner of my eye, I saw one of Shane's sisters walking around in circles in the field with her face buried in her hands, inconsolable in her grief. I will never forget the heart-wrenching sounds that filled the field. My body didn't feel the pain—I could only hear it.

I clearly remember lying in the emergency room, waiting to be seen by a doctor, and saying to myself, This is the worst thing that will ever happen to me. I will never get over this.

My parents came to the hospital as soon as they got the early-morning phone call. I can still see my father standing at the end of the bed with tears streaming down his face. He couldn't speak. I must have looked terrible, black and blue with a scissor cut across my face. I didn't want to see myself and didn't look in a mirror until three weeks later, when I got home. No one could believe it. It was all too much to take in. Pete was dead. He had taken the full impact of the crash and died instantly. Thank goodness, Shane survived. He suffered a severe concussion and broken leg. He had no recollection of traveling from London, the accident, or our phone call. It would be years before I would be able to feel the full impact of the collision.

I never did go to New York that summer. I missed my last semester in college, stayed at home, and learned how to walk again. My pelvis was fractured, and there was severe damage to my right foot and left hand. The jagged scar over my lip remains a constant reminder of that night. Shane stayed home, too. In my mind, I kept protesting that our relationship was over but was too afraid to say it out loud, as I knew it would sound terrible to everyone. He needed me now more than ever. I didn't want him to need me. I didn't want this tragic, freak accident to mark and map out the rest of my life. I felt so much pressure from him and his family and from what I thought people would think. Pressure to stay with him and support him.

I had a summer full of guilt and remorse for wanting nothing to do with Shane. What was wrong with me? How could I be so cruel? I thought if I could just get out of Ireland, I could forget about all this trauma, forget about Pete dying, forget about the drunk driver who hit us, forget about the scar on the side of my face, forget about the boyfriend who needed me now more than ever, forget that I felt guilty for not wanting to be with him, forget that I blamed myself.

I felt responsible for Pete's death. If only I hadn't broken it off with Shane on the phone, if only Pete took his motorbike instead of driving us all in his car, if only I wasn't in such a bad mood, then maybe it never would have happened. The *if onlys* haunted me like ghosts. I couldn't express my anguish and torment, because I didn't know how. My family and friends didn't know how to express theirs either. So we didn't. I kept all the confused emotions and feelings of guilt, grief, anger, fear, and helplessness inside me and focused on studying for my exams in September. I naively believed that my plans would save me. My plans would carry me through the next year of college, until I could leave and put all of this behind me. Once and for all.

I decided to wait until the end of the summer to tell Shane I couldn't be his girlfriend anymore. It was extremely hard for me to go through with it and I felt terrible, but it was my life, and I wanted to get on with it. He didn't take it well, neither did his family. The gossip was terrible—in my mind at least. I imagined people were talking behind my back in the village pub saying what a bitch I was for leaving him, and some people surely were. But for the first time in my life, I didn't care what people said, and I didn't let it stop me. I was twenty years old, and the only thing I thought I had to hold on to was a future I could plan and dream about.

Shane visited me the following Easter, on the anniversary of the accident. I still had feelings for him and still felt guilty for abandoning him when he needed me. I wanted to be friends, to ease my conscience. We had goodbye sex one last time, just before I left for New York. I had no idea at the time that my "one big event" was the start of a collision course with everything I thought about life, myself, my values, my beliefs, and my dreams.

When I started therapy, I was new to the whole mind, body, spirit interplay and did not make any connection between my emotions and my body. The more I talked with Freda, the more curious I got about it. Where did all the trauma and pain go? Where did all the sorrow go? I thought if I consciously remembered and tried to deal with my pain and emotions, maybe my body would be able to let go of it, and I could forget.

In the past, it had always been too painful to remember. When the uncomfortable memories and emotions started to arise, I would quickly push them away and distract myself with something else. The distractions varied over the years. Initially, the first summer after the car crash, I threw myself into studying and fighting with my mother and sister. Atop the long list of evasions during my twenties and early thirties were eating, television, working, shopping, drinking, smoking, and socializing—basically, all of the activities that made up my life! At least, the life I thought

I was supposed to be living. It seemed to be what everyone else was doing too.

When I started seeing Freda after my second incidence of cancer, it was the beginning of a whole new relationship with myself. Our weekly meetings started the long, slow, and sometimes painful process of being willing to ask questions and get curious about the uncomfortable feelings and memories I had done my best to avoid my whole life. I started to see that I really hadn't or couldn't push the pain and trauma away. I'd only pushed them underneath, into the dark and sleeping parts of my consciousness, where they laid festering like unhealed wounds, waiting to reveal themselves in all kinds of ways that were not easily recognizable and that I didn't understand.

For years afterward, I was afraid to drive in the dark. That one fear was easily recognizable, and I eventually overcame it by rationalizing and practicing driving at night in the presence of compassionate copilots. Some of the other effects of the accident were subtler and took me years to recognize. The accident had confirmed some deep-rooted, unconscious beliefs I'd been carrying around since childhood. One unconscious belief was: if I speak out and make a fuss, something terrible will happen. I may have picked that one up by witnessing my father's short temper when I talked back as a child. In any case, when I spoke my mind and broke it off with Shane, something terrible did happen. Of course, I wasn't aware of that connection then or that I even held that belief. I also wasn't aware of the enormous amount of power I was giving to myself by carrying that belief around.

Rather than face the consequences of speaking my mind, which I often did not have the self-confidence to do anyway, it was far easier to go with the flow, so as not to make a scene and rock the boat. It has only been by taking a step back—observing my behavior over the years and experiencing the consequences of decisions I was unable to make—that I can even see it now.

I may not have wanted the car accident to leave a mark on my life, but it did leave its marks physically, mentally, and emotionally. The more I tried to deny the effects, the harder I needed to compensate to cover them up. When I started to get curious about them in therapy and ask some questions, they slowly started to resurface, and I was able to tend to them and begin to let them go. Talking about it in therapy was only the beginning, though. It would be another ten years before I would fully be able to connect with the sleeping giants of anger, rage, and grief that were buried deep inside me and finally allow them to rise entirely to consciousness.

Over the years, I had often wondered about the young woman whose soothing voice and compassionate hand reached into the car to comfort me that night. I never knew who it was. Then, just a couple of years ago, on a visit back home, twenty years after the car accident, my sister-in-law casually said that Mary Ryan often asked after me.

"Who?"

"The woman who came upon the car accident."

It turned out Mary was a neighbor of my sister-in-law's family, who lived in a small village five miles away. I wanted to meet her. I wanted to ask her questions and thank her for being so kind. She told me she was on her way home with her boyfriend, from the same venue, when they came upon the accident. It was a three-car pileup. The fierce impact of the crash forced Pete's little Ford Fiesta off the road and into a nearby field. I wanted to know everything she could remember.

After we spoke for a while, I realized we had different versions of the same night. There were different details that we remembered, and of course, we were carrying around different stories. I have no doubt that everyone involved in the accident has a different story that is true and personal to them—just like siblings brought up together in the same house have wildly different versions and experiences of what growing up was like.

After I spoke to Mary, it was clear to me that I needed to be willing to let go of my story. I wanted to become bigger than the story so that the story, the fear, the pain, and the memory didn't identify me and control the rest of my life. It is still painful to remember. I am still letting go. It took me years to realize that I am bigger than the fears and the uncomfortable feelings that the car accident marked me with; today I can say that they don't control my life anymore.

Over the years, I have had to let go of my childhood story that one big thing happens to everybody. There is no one big thing. Life is the big thing that is going on all the time.

CHAPTER

5

Secrets and Shadows

One word frees us of all the weight and pain of life:
That word is love.

—SOPHOCLES

I had been in New York for about two weeks when I noticed that my period was late. It was the summer of 1988, and I had just graduated from college in Ireland. I couldn't wait to leave Ireland behind and start my new life and new journey up the corporate ladder. That was all I ever thought about in my senior year at Waterford Institute of Technology, then known by the far less sophisticated name of Waterford Regional Technical College. While fellow students were wondering what jobs they would apply for, and where they could apprentice as accountants, I was wondering what day I could fly away and leave Ireland.

Two days after my final economics paper was handed in, I packed my few belongings, which included one new suit, and headed for my cousin Rosie's apartment in the Irish neighborhood in the Bronx where I grew up. I had stayed there a couple of summers before, and Rosie agreed I could stay until I got on my feet. My plan was to land a fabulous, well-paying job on Wall Street, find my own place in Manhattan as soon as possible, and kiss my old life goodbye. Illusions of grandeur fueled all my plans.

I was twenty-one years old, I wanted to be successful, and I was anxious to get started.

When I arrived in New York and started applying for jobs, I was shocked to be told that I had no office skills and was not very employable. In my innocence and arrogance, I thought typing, switchboards, and fax machines were for secretaries. I had a business degree, for God's sake. I didn't need to know how to do those things, right? According to the headhunters, temp agencies, and employers, however, I was wrong. In addition, no one had ever heard of Waterford Regional Technical College, and as far as potential employers were concerned, I was an Irish girl just off the boat. One recruitment agent even asked me if I'd ever thought about becoming a nanny, as the pay would probably be better than the office jobs he was putting me forward for. No!

My ideas about myself and what I could actually do didn't match the positions or the salaries that were being offered. So I panicked. I took the first job that was offered to me, as an assistant in the marine department of an insurance brokerage firm. This involved rating insurance policies, sending lots of faxes, filing lots of files, and answering the phone. I figured everyone had to start somewhere, so I took the job. Months later, I found a waitress job at night to help subsidize my meager salary. It wasn't quite the sophisticated start I had imagined, but I assured myself that it was temporary. I would do it until something better came along.

I didn't think too much about it when my period was late, as I had been under a lot of stress and pressure in the two weeks since I had arrived in New York. That must have been the reason. There was no way I could be pregnant. Girls like me didn't get pregnant. I didn't sleep around. I only ever had one "real" boyfriend since I was sixteen, not counting the few dates here and there, in between breaking up and making up with Shane. It just wasn't possible.

Girls like me did not get pregnant before they were married. I couldn't even bear to imagine it. What would everyone think? I was the oldest daughter of devout Irish-Catholic parents and the first person to go to college in my family. My life was just starting!

I bought a pregnancy test for ten dollars in a drugstore downtown, on my way home from work. I peed on the stick to reassure myself that this was a false alarm. Then I stared at the pink plus sign on the plastic stick in disbelief for a minute or two—shit, I was pregnant!—before I decided that I would never tell anyone. Not a soul. I made my decision before it ever occurred to me that there were options, that I had a choice. As far as I was concerned, there was no choice, there was no room for this in my life. It was not part of the plan. Girls like me did not get pregnant.

I clearly remember sitting alone at the kitchen table and touching my belly with both hands. There was a baby growing inside me. I allowed myself to love it for less than one minute, and then I cried from the pit of my stomach. I cried and cried, and when I wiped away my tears, I promised myself never to feel the intensity of that love and that pain again.

The next day, I knew I had to do something fast to "take care of it." I phoned Shane in Dublin and told him I was pregnant. He did his best to convince me that I couldn't possibly be. I assured him I had already gone through all of that already and that the pink sign on the stick confirmed it was true. He told me he knew I had plans, which did not include a baby, and he would send me money to "take care of it." It wasn't a part of his plan either, but he never said so.

Neither of us ever mentioned the word *abortion*. It was too crass, too real, and illegal in Ireland. It was something neither of us ever imagined would happen to us. Our big life event, the car accident, had already happened. This was just bad luck. No one would ever need to know. I made him promise he would never tell anyone and never to speak to me of it ever again. For years afterward, I worried about whether Shane ever told anyone.

The next day, on the way to work, I saw an advertisement for an abortion clinic on the subway car of the number 4 train that went to Wall Street from Woodlawn station in the Bronx. My stop was Fulton Street, the one just before Wall Street. I worked on the 102nd floor of the World Trade Center. The sign was in Spanish, but it was pretty obvious what it was for. When I thought no one was looking, I wrote down the phone number on a crumpled up piece of tissue in my pocket. I called on my lunch break, gave a false name, and made an appointment to visit the clinic the following Saturday. I was worried about missing work. The lady on the phone told me I would be a little sore for a few days afterward, but I should be fine to go to work on Monday. I was relieved. It would cost two hundred dollars. Cash would be best. I could be in and out in a few hours. No one would ever have to know—no one—especially not my mom and dad.

I felt so full of shame on the cab ride to the clinic. I could still hardly believe that I was pregnant. I kept telling myself that I had no choice and this was the only thing to do. I knew I was committing a grave sin. The nuns at the Presentation Convent had made that very clear to us in religion class. There was no doubt about it, I was going straight to hell for this, but in that moment I didn't care. I would deal with hell later; now I needed to make sure that I took care of the pregnancy without anyone ever knowing. After it was all over, I could put it behind me, charge full speed ahead with my plans, and pretend it never happened.

When I arrived at the clinic, the lady at the front desk asked me if I had seen a doctor. I hadn't, so she asked me to pee into a cup and then, a few minutes later, confirmed that I was six-weeks pregnant. I filled out all the paperwork, using my false name, and handed over the cash. It occurred to me, if something went wrong and I died, how would anyone ever know it was me?

The nurse handed me a short white gown to change into, and gave me a basket with a number on it for my clothes. I walked down the corridor to the dismal changing room that looked like a gymnasium locker room with rows of benches and anonymous, numbered steel lockers. My hands trembled as I took off each piece of familiar clothing, and I was afraid that I was going to throw up.

The waiting room was full of gray plastic chairs in a huge circle, and every chair was occupied. The room was packed with at least fifty young women, mostly Hispanic and African American. There were no men in sight. All of us were wearing the same short, white medical gown with two little strings in the back keeping it all together. I couldn't help noticing that I was the only white girl in the room, but I was not the only one crying. The girl next to me told me it was her fourth abortion and that I should shut up crying, because it was no big deal. I did shut up crying, and I never cried about it again until five years later.

Despite feeling sore, I went out later that night and started drinking and smoking and eating. I continued to drink and smoke and eat, and ended up gaining thirty pounds in the next six months—probably the same amount of weight I would have gained had I remained pregnant. Instead of carrying a baby in my belly, I carried thirty pounds of guilt and shame and a whole lot of unconscious pain. I did not have any boyfriends for a couple of years, and I am guessing I sent out an unconscious signal: I am not worthy, stay away from me.

I joined Weight Watchers after my Aunt Mary told me, in her heavy Irish accent, "You are a disgrace! You are fat and you need to get a grip!" As furious as I was with her, I knew she was right. So I got a grip on my plans again, which included fitting into my work clothes and moving up the corporate ladder. This entailed moving to London eighteen months later, away from the place of my terrible secret.

The memories of that day, sitting in a gray plastic chair and pretending to be somebody else, resurfaced five years later when I was sitting at my kitchen table with Tess in a flat in North London. After the first time I found out I had breast cancer, Tess came over to talk to me. She was the best friend of my two cousins, Marie and Eileen. They grew up in North London together. We all had something in common. We all had Irish parents, moved to Ireland just around puberty, and went to high schools run by nuns. And we all left Ireland after college. Tess was an art teacher and someone with whom I loved to spend time. She was fun and wise and creative. Tess had cancer when she a kid. She never talked about it, but when she heard my news she immediately came around to visit. It was good to see her, as she was always so full of life and stories. We sat in the kitchen and talked.

I told everyone else how fine I was, that there was no need to worry, but it was different with Tess, because she had been through it. I told her how afraid I was. I was afraid of the anesthetic, afraid that I would never wake up. I was afraid of chemo, afraid that I would be throwing up all the time, and afraid that I'd lose my hair. I was afraid that the Scottish boyfriend I was living with would not be able to cope and would leave me. I was afraid of people knowing. I seemed to be afraid of everything. For hours, I let it all pour out to Tess, all my fears.

Except one.

My biggest fear was that God was punishing me for having had an abortion. I never said it out loud, but she seemed to know somehow. After talking with me for hours, she looked me in the eye and said, "You did nothing to deserve this. You are not being punished. It is not your fault. God loves you."

"God loves me." Where did that come from? I'd never heard Tess talk about God before. When she said this, a flood of tears came pouring out, followed by a confession (not to a priest in a box, but to Tess at the kitchen table), along with the relief of not having to hold the secret by myself anymore. In that moment, I wanted to believe her. Maybe God loved me. But I did not love me—that was the problem.

Over the years, I have written in my journals and talked to numerous friends and therapists. I don't think I deserved to get cancer. I don't believe anyone does. Nonetheless, for twenty years, I continued holding ceremonies and fire rituals by myself, trying to let go of the shame and the pain around the decision I made when I was twenty-one. A few years ago, I finally told my mother during a visit to Ireland. She hadn't known. I told her what happened, explained why I needed to write about it, and said I hoped she would understand. She showed me the love that was always there, just waiting for me to accept it, and expressed how sorry she was that I'd had to go through it alone.

It took several more years to realize that there was another piece of the story I had not ever dared to go near—Dad. I was sure my father would never understand. In fact, when I look back on it now, I think it was his disapproval and disappointment in me that I feared the most. I had always wanted him to think I was good; I wanted him to be proud of me. Now I know he always was. He just didn't know how to express it.

Throughout my life, whenever I told my dad I loved him, his response was always, "The same to you." This usually drove me crazy and sent me ranting and raving to my mom, who would just smile and assure me that he did love me, he just couldn't say it. My father was born in 1939 into a rural, working-class, Irish-Catholic family, where expressing emotions was never a part of daily life.

I, on the other hand, had grown up in 1970s America, watching *The Brady Bunch* and *Little House on the Prairie,* where the dads were always saying "I love you" to their kids. After years of doing the same dance with my dad, I finally broke the code. "Did you change the oil in your car?" really meant, "I love you with all of my heart, and I always will."

My dad died last year after a long and brave battle with Parkinson's disease. It is one of the greatest blessings of my life that I was with him when he crossed over. I was living halfway across the world, and I know he waited to die for me to travel back to Ireland to be with him. He loved me. He always loved me, even when I thought his love should look and sound different than it did. In the days leading up to his death, all the stories I had been carrying around for years just fell away. All that was left was love. There was only love. It had always been there underneath the disappointments, misunderstandings, and miscommunications of a lifetime.

I never told Dad about the abortion. He would have disapproved. But after all those years, I finally knew nothing could ever have stopped him from loving me. I was his daughter, after all. Nine days after Dad died, I asked him for his forgiveness—not for having had an abortion—I asked him to forgive me for ever having doubted his love for me, just like I asked God to forgive me for doubting Her love. Then I was able to forgive myself.

I don't believe God punishes us; I believe we punish ourselves.

My guilt and shame stopped me from having a voice. Guilt and shame silence many women. The secret abortion has been part of my shadow for most of my adult life. Abortion is not my shadow alone. Nations have shadows too. When a shadow is not owned, it is projected onto some else. Shadows are dangerous when they are ignored.

Over the years, countless numbers of women have boarded boats and sailed across the wild and dark Irish Sea to England, to end pregnancies that they didn't want or were too ashamed to carry. It is a painful decision that no woman makes lightly. Once "taken care of," they get the boat back to Ireland. The boats have not yet been burned. So there is no smoke. No shadow to look at and inquire into. No conversation. Today, abortion is still illegal in Ireland, and women still do not have a choice. It is a controversial and painful issue for many people to discuss. One day the boats, full of secrets and projections, need to be burned so the smoke can lift. Then, maybe, a nation can see and hear all of her daughters.

There are "girls like me" everywhere: girls who lack self-confidence and self-esteem; girls who think they have to live their life a certain way to be respected and loved; girls who secretly think they are not enough. If we could only love ourselves the way God loves us, ours would be a different story and a different world. The question is: why don't we?

The first time I got breast cancer, I thought it was because of the abortion. The second time, I thought it was because of the car accident.

The third time, I had no idea—but I knew it was time to get creative.

CHAPTER

6

Surrendering
to the Unknown

*And the time came when the risk to remain tight
in a bud was more painful than the risk it took to
blossom.*

—ANAÏS NIN

My creative recovery started in front of the television. The ritual was the same every day: breakfast at the kitchen table, watching *Richard and Judy* (Britain's version of *The Today Show*, if it were combined with *Kelly and Michael*), followed by a plethora of other talk shows I can't even remember. All the chatting and channel flicking led up to the highlight of the day: *Oprah*.

The Oprah Winfrey Show was my savior during my first few months of being at home after the third cancer diagnosis. I would honor the occasion each day by moving from the kitchen table to the living room couch. Mom almost always joined me for *Oprah*, often bringing in a pot of tea with freshly baked scones and jam. She knew how much I looked forward to the program, and more than anything, it was something else for us to focus on. Monday through Friday, we would sit, listen, and comment on Oprah's various guests and their sensational stories, and I would try to block out thoughts of the future, which always filled me with fear and worry.

Initially, I was full of self-judgment for spending my days in front of the television set. I thought I should be taking the opportunity to improve myself, read the classics, and accomplish something important. After all, I'd never had time to do those things before. I was always so busy: busy working, socializing, shopping—go, go, go—busy keeping myself busy. No time to slow down. So lying on the couch for hours, days, and weeks at a time was foreign to me. Before, I'd always had to be doing something. The truth was that I was now too wiped to do anything else, with the one exception of receiving my weekly Reiki treatments. Tuning into other people's lives on the television served as a temporary escape from my own. I was afraid to make a move. What if it was in the wrong direction? Although I knew I couldn't stay in front of the television forever, those few months spent watching daytime television were a huge source of comfort for me. I felt safe on the couch.

I watched the breaking news of Princess Diana's tragic death on the TV, saw replays of her car accident, and wept in shock along with everybody else. Diana's death affected me far more than I would have expected. I was heartbroken. How could someone so young and attractive, with her whole life ahead of her, die so suddenly? I told myself I was crying for Diana.

"That lad had cancer three times too. Look at him now. Isn't he great!" Mom said, pointing to the television emphatically. We roared at the TV, jumping up and down as we saw Lance Armstrong whiz past the finish line of the Tour de France in his yellow jersey. If Lance could win the Tour de France—the most grueling and challenging bike race in the world—after three bouts with cancer, surely to God I could do something too. Couldn't I? Tears roll down my face as I remember how much hope I was filled with that day. Now, I am saddened as I learn of Lance's fall from grace and his ban from professional sports due to performance-enhancing drug use. Yet I am still grateful for the seed of possibility that was planted in me then.

One day, three weeks before my chemo was about to start, I sat upright on the couch and announced to myself, "I am going to embrace this cancer creatively." I never considered myself a creative person. I had, however, harbored secret fantasies of playing guitar and singing in an all-girl rock band, since I was in high school. The reality of my not being able to play the guitar, or sing for that matter (I knew the chorus to almost every song, though), were minor details. I imagined myself speaking Spanish fluently, conversing with my guides in Peru as they led me to the top of Machu Picchu, which I would climb effortlessly. I had never gotten around to taking a Spanish class or buying a pair of hiking boots, but I was determined that all those things would change. My newfound creativity would include learning to ride horses, speak new languages, play instruments, design and make jewelry—for starters! Most of those things are now a part of my life. However, they have all taken different forms and much longer to get around to than I ever could have imagined back then. But I held them in my heart, until I eventually got around to them.

As for embracing cancer creatively, I had no idea what that was supposed to look like, other than these sudden bursts of inspiration to learn and do new things. I felt the place to start might be with my hair loss, as it was the next part of the cancer treatment that was facing me. I didn't want it to be one more thing that was happening to me; I wanted to feel like I was involved in the process. I wanted to participate in it.

Except for that one really bad haircut just before my prom, I'd always had long auburn hair. My long and unruly hair was a part of my identity. It was how people often described me, a trademark of sorts. My oncologist advised me that once the chemo began my hair could start falling out at any time. He didn't know when it would start or how long it would take, he just knew that it would all fall out sooner or later due to the aggressive type of chemo I was prescribed.

My family and friends were all freaked out by the thought of me losing my hair. It scared me too. It was unknown territory. But the recent loss of my right breast was more of a concern to me. I was thirty-one years old and single. Who would ever want me now? Of course, my family and friends didn't have to see that or deal with it. That loss could be disguised. The prosthesis, handed to me upon leaving the hospital, took care of that. All I had to do was insert it into my empty bra cup. No one would ever know one breast was fake and detachable. My hair loss was a different story. This meant I would look like I had cancer.

A well-meaning friend from college, who was rapidly rising to great heights in the Dublin public relations scene, suggested we go wig shopping one afternoon. The idea of wearing a wig did not appeal to me. She thought it would be easier for me if I didn't look like I had cancer. I wasn't sure about that, but I was sure that it would be easier for her. I didn't want to hide from the fact that I had cancer again. Mostly, I didn't want to hide from myself anymore. The first two times, I never looked like I had cancer, so I pretended I didn't and just got on with it. I wanted the third time to be different. I wanted it to be the last time. I didn't want to cover up and pretend it wasn't happening. I did that before, and cancer kept coming back. I felt that if I could face it and not hide from it, maybe I could be rid of it.

Despite my uneasiness with the whole wig thing, I reluctantly tried on a few new do's, mainly to get my friend "out of my hair." There were only two wig shops to choose from in Dublin, and one of them doubled as a costume store. After fifteen minutes in the first shop, it was clear I looked ridiculous as Cher, Stevie Nicks, Elvis, and Bob Marley. We abandoned the wig search, went to McDaid's Pub, and had a good laugh over a glass of Guinness. My pal agreed I might as well look like I had cancer, as myself. We raised our glasses and toasted to it.

The next day, I made an appointment to get my hair cut at a salon off Grafton Street, the trendy part of Dublin where all the artsy people got their hair cut. I thought it would be easier to deal with my hair falling out if it was short. I told the stylist what was happening and asked him to give me a super-trendy, super-stylish, super-short cut. I gave him full permission to be as creative as he liked. He must have thought it was Christmas, as he dived in with his super-sharp scissors. With each snip, a part of my old identity hit the floor.

I only let myself feel sad for a moment. A trendy hair salon is no place for tears, I told myself and then pulled it together. I kept my eyes closed for the duration of the entire haircut and imagined that letting go of my hair was letting go of everything that could no longer help me, everything inauthentic about me—a shedding of all the masks, as my Reiki therapist Karen would say. I thought of that first Reiki session at the holistic fair, just before my mastectomy, where Karen explained that the strange sensation I was feeling in my face during the session was all the masks coming off. I didn't have to be afraid. I felt lighter.

When I opened my eyes, I was still there. My hair was just shorter, and I liked it. I was the same; you could just see more of me. My hair was not me! It felt empowering to participate in my hair loss, rather than feeling like it was another thing that was happening to me.

I was still nervous about how I would feel when my hair did start falling out. Another good friend from college, Lucia, suggested a group of us go down to West Cork for a few days, to get my mind off of it. That seemed like an excellent plan. West Cork, as all my friends know, is one of my favorite places in Ireland, maybe even the world. It is wild, remote, mystical, and magical—the westernmost part of Europe. Artists, musicians, farmers, and every kind of healer you can imagine populate the area. It has long been a place of refuge for me.

The five-hour drive down from Dublin took us as far away from the office and city life as we could get. It felt like the strong Atlantic wind could magically carry my troubles away, for the time I was there, at least. The first morning I woke up in the bed–and–breakfast, a clump of auburn hair lay on my pillow. I felt sick to my stomach. More came out in the shower, and the bar of soap looked like a mouse in my hand: My head was not the only place that lost hair. It seemed every time I touched my head that morning, more hair came out.

Lucia was sharing the room with me and made a feeble attempt to convince me that it didn't look that bad. "Come on, Lucia, it looks awful. I'll have a comb-over by the end of the day. Give me a break!" I said. Then she started laughing and apologizing for laughing between guffaws. I couldn't believe it. "Why the hell are you laughing? This is serious. I look like a freak!" Then I started laughing. I did look kind of funny. The funniest part of all was that a part of myself that I identified with so strongly my whole life had just fallen down the shower drain, and I was still there—and I was fine.

It was time to get creative with my new look. I folded over a beautiful, multicolored silk scarf that I purchased the previous day in one of the cute, local art shops. I played with it until it looked like it belonged on my head. Then I put on a pair of long, dangling earrings, applied an extra coat of mascara, and went down to the beach. When I got home a few days later, I shaved off the remaining tufts of hair. Shaving my head was one of the most liberating things I had ever done. I felt free. I also felt a little bit like Sinead O'Connor, the controversial Irish rock star who chose to shave off her hair in the 1980s and has been sporting a bald head for years. For me, Sinead's bald head was a symbol of a woman who was not afraid to be seen and heard as herself. In my opinion, Sinead O'Connor kicked ass!

Unfortunately, as the weeks passed, the only ass I was kicking was my own. There were two weeks between each chemotherapy session where I felt reasonably good and one week when I felt like shit. That was my week on the couch with the TV. After the first round of chemo, I got off my own back and gave myself permission to surrender and not do anything for that week. The less I fought the tiredness and sick feeling, the better I felt. Surrendering was not in my nature, so I was surprised how good it felt when I let go of how I thought I was supposed to look, feel, and recover. I was not surrendering to the cancer. I was surrendering to the unknown. I wanted to listen. I felt in my heart the cancer was trying to tell me something.

I felt so much turmoil inside, and I did not know what to do with it. One part of me wanted to surrender. Another part wanted to fight and know what was going to happen next. I thought if I could let go of having to know, like I let go of my hair, something new and amazing might rise up to meet me. There seemed to be so many contradictions inside me, and they showed up in how I was living. For example, my work life and personal life were totally separate. They even had different names. Margaret was my official work name, and Peggy was my name for everything else. It was reminiscent of the confusion I'd felt on reaching Ireland and having my mother tell me I shouldn't use my name, Peggy, in school (though I did, despite her instruction).

My first memory of ever being called Margaret was on my first day of school, which was also my fifth birthday. Miss Rosenstock, my kindergarten teacher, called me Margaret, just like Mom said she would. The night before school started, Mom explained that everyone at school would call me Margaret, because it was my "real" name. Peggy was my nickname for outside of school—and later on, for outside of work. Margaret and Peggy were different in the way they moved in the world, and I kept them that way. Separate. It didn't feel safe for one to cross over into the other's territory.

I realize now that feeling arose from a serious lack of self-confidence, which I had so cleverly disguised as suit-clad Margaret in the city, and as fun-loving-hippy-chick Peggy in North London or wherever else I was living. I always had the sinking feeling that I wouldn't be able to pull either persona off completely. Not smart enough, not creative enough, not good enough—not enough, full stop. As much as I disliked my work, it was what I knew, which made me comfortable and uncomfortable at the same time. My boss was genuinely kind and understanding, and I was reassured I could take as much time off as I needed. How long would that last, I wondered. I couldn't imagine going back to the office and being Margaret ever again. I had already been off for two months. How much more time could I take? Why did I get cancer again? What was I doing wrong? What was my true identity? How would I make a living? Would I ever meet a man? It was a minefield, in my mind at least, and I didn't know what to do.

I was tired of trying to figure it all out in my head. Nothing made sense anymore. I wanted to place the confusion and struggle outside of me, so I could step back and see it. Maybe then I could begin to have a creative relationship with it and stop reacting from the past, from what I already knew. In a desperate longing to make sense of how I was feeling, I decided to paint. Freda, my therapist, had suggested I try painting before, but I'd always come back with the same excuse: not enough time. This time, I had no excuse. I was desperate and I was ready.

The decision to paint was a big deal for me. I hadn't picked up a paintbrush since kindergarten, and I assumed painting was for really cool people who knew what they were doing. I certainly did not feel cool, and I had no idea what I was doing. Painting was unknown territory.

In my late twenties, I was introduced to *Women Who Run with the Wolves* by Clarissa Pinkola Estés. It is a thick and powerful book, full of myths and stories of the wild woman archetype, which invites us to bring alive that which is sleeping in our souls. I'd long intended to read it, but I was always too busy. Now that I was too tired to be too busy, I picked it up and started reading. I was intrigued by the stories and how familiar they felt to me, even though I hadn't heard them before. I was also intrigued by the image on the cover, which had an ancient and primordial feel to it. There is a golden crescent moon in the dark blue background. There are two naked figures running across a desert terrain. One is dark orange and the other an indigo blue. Their arms are outstretched. One is looking back at the other. It is not clear what is going on between them. It looks like they are running in the dark. I immediately identified with the separateness of the two figures, the sense of struggle, and the running. When I turned the book over and discovered the painting, by Eileen Cooper, was titled "All Hell Broke Loose," I knew I wanted to begin by copying that painting. The only problem was, I did not know how to start.

I didn't want that to stop me from trying, as it had in the past. So I called my friend Fiona, who loves art, and asked her for help. She was more than happy to get me started. I was thirty-one years old and had never set foot in an art supply store before. Procrastination was my art form of choice. My fear of "not getting it right" and thinking I was supposed to know what I wanted before I went in had always stopped me from entering in the past. I didn't feel the same way about other stores, which my credit card reflected, but there was something about "art" and "art stores" that intimidated me. I was embarrassed to tell Fiona. I thought it sounded lame and silly. When I told her I was nervous and scared about painting, she didn't think it was silly, she understood. To my surprise, she told me she felt nervous every time she was about to start a new art project. I asked why and she replied, "I know it's going to change me in some way." I totally got it. As much as I craved change, the thought of it also scared me. Enough procrastinating; it was time to begin.

We decided to make a day out of it and arranged to meet in Dublin for lunch. I always loved dressing up and decided to dress appropriately for the big occasion. In the weeks following my hair loss, I tried to get creative with my new look as much as possible. I bought different colored scarves and a few cute hats to play with. This day, I carefully chose a batik-dyed long dress that I'd picked up on sale the week before while shopping with my mom, donned a pair of large silver hoop earrings, applied some dramatic eye makeup, and topped my outfit off with a black-rimmed cotton hat with a white flower on it. I figured if I didn't feel like an artist, I could at least look like one. As I was getting ready, it occurred to me I had done the same thing with work. I traveled to work every day dressed up in my suit and heels, with my makeup and hair just right, clutching my briefcase. I always looked the part.

Over lunch, I showed the image I intended to paint to Fiona. I could tell by her reaction that she was curious about why I was so drawn to paint it, as I admit it was a bit strange looking. I shared how conflicted I felt between my work life and personal life. I didn't want to go back to work, but I didn't know how to leave and move forward either. Fiona was surprised to hear me say that, as she always saw me as fun, creative, and full of life. I am generously guessing that my coworkers would have been surprised too, as at work I was ambitious, conscientious, and got along with most people. No one knew how trapped and confused I was feeling inside. I could talk about it, complain about it, and joke about it, but I didn't know what to do about it. For some reason I am still not sure of, I thought painting the image might help.

With Fiona by my side, the art store felt more like a candy store. Fiona filled me in on a few basics to consider when choosing a type of paint. I went with acrylics, as she described acrylic as the most forgiving of paints. It dries quickly and you can paint over it again and again and again. Forgiving sounded good to me. There were so many choices to make, and it was all so new. What size, color, texture of paper? What kind of brushes? What colors to buy? It was so exciting, and I gave myself permission to enjoy not knowing how it would turn out, instead of worrying about how good it would be. I was doing it for myself, no one else.

It took me two hours to drive back home from Dublin. During the drive, I kept looking in my rearview mirror to admire the newly acquired art supplies that filled up the backseat of my little red Ford Fiesta. I was proud of the array of colors that peeked through the bags when I turned a corner or stopped at a light. I was going to paint! I was excited as I drove up to my parents' house. I couldn't wait to get started.

I taped the huge roll of thick white paper to my brothers' old bedroom wall, pushed the bureau to the side, threw an old yellow sheet over the blue carpet, and declared it my new art studio. My makeshift canvas measured four by six feet, framed by the cream-colored masking tape that kept it stuck to the wall. The first part was easy. Fiona advised I apply several coats of white paint to prep the paper before I started working with the colors. I am not sure if there was a technical reason for this, but dipping the paintbrush into the white paint can over and over again and brushing it onto the paper with wide, long strokes felt good. This was my blank canvas, my fresh start, just like my bald head. I was prepping myself, as well as the paper, for the new relationship I was about to enter with myself.

Once the canvas was ready, I put on some music and lit a candle. I chose Sinead O'Connor's album *Universal Mother.* I dipped the paintbrush into the midnight blue paint, listened to the music, closed my eyes, and entered into the unknown. I kept telling myself it didn't matter what the painting looked like, only how it felt. I reminded myself there was no rush, no deadline, and nothing to accomplish. I took my time. I felt my way into it.

Over the weeks and months, as the layers of paint slowly went on, my relationship with the image started to change. At first, I saw the two figures as Margaret and Peggy, separate: one running away from the other, one trying to catch up with the other; one trying to have a good time, the other trying to stop it; one fun, the other serious; one flaky, the other industrious. Later, I saw them as masculine and feminine parts of myself. The interpretations were endless, and my opinions and judgments of my painting fluctuated depending on the situation. But one thing remained constant: as long as the two characters, which I identified as different parts of myself, were disconnected, it was exhausting. The amount of energy required to fuel both and keep them both running separately ensured that I was running on empty.

With each layer of paint, the image invited me to go deeper, beyond the surface of what I could see. I began to get in touch with the pain that was being mirrored back to me and that was inside of me—the pain of separation. I understood it was not the cancer that was trying to tell me something, it was my soul. My soul was crying out to me to stop, to listen, and to pay attention to how I was feeling.

Something new wanted to emerge. I didn't know what it was at the time, but I trusted it. I started to feel compassion toward myself for the hard time I'd been giving myself my whole life, thinking I had to be one way or another, feeling like I was never enough. I empathized with the two figures and wanted to bring them together inside me. It was the start of a long process of integration—integrating the parts of myself that felt disconnected and at odds.

In the meantime, the painting caused a lot of excitement in the house. My nephews, Danny and Brian, who were four and five years old, would excitedly run upstairs every time to see the two "lads" with their bare backsides. The creatures on the huge paper canvas fascinated them, and they always wanted to paint. In fact, I did let them paint on the first few layers with me, and then Mom and I set up canvases for them to paint alongside me. I wanted to include my family in my recovery, this time in a way that would not be threatening to them. We were not the type of family who sat around the dinner table and discussed how we were feeling.

The painting turned out to be a lifeline for all of us that summer. It stayed taped to the wall for eight months, during all of my chemotherapy treatments. My father made a beautiful oak frame for it with his own two hands. My brothers carried it downstairs, and my mother proudly hung it in the living room, where it took up an entire wall. They embraced the painting—as strange as it must have looked to them—with the same quiet strength and kindness they embraced me with during those months on the couch.

Shaving my head and painting were my first crucial steps in a creative "uncovering." As the layers of paint went on the blank canvas, it was like the layers of the image I had of myself were being peeled away, like an onion. It was the start of recognizing and loosening my grip on the rigid identities that kept me stuck not feeling good enough. I wondered what was underneath my image, underneath the hair, clothes, names, and ideas I had about who I was. Why didn't I feel whole, why wasn't I happy, what was missing? What was underneath all those identities I had been carrying around my whole life? I didn't have answers. I knew I wasn't my hair or my breast or my name or my job, so who was I, and why did I keep getting cancer? All I knew was that I needed to go deeper—all hell had broken loose—even though I was afraid of what I might discover.

CHAPTER

7

Living the Questions

*I want to beg you, to be patient toward all that is
unsolved in your heart and try to love the questions
themselves like locked rooms and like books that
are written in a very foreign tongue. Do not now
seek the answers, which cannot be given you because
you would not be able to live them. And the point
is to live everything.*

—Rainer Maria Rilke

A few days after hearing the news of my third cancer, I phoned the institute in Dublin where the psychotherapy training course was due to start in September. I was nervous to tell them I would be having chemotherapy treatments throughout the first year of the course, afraid they would no longer accept me. To my relief and surprise, the director's response was positive. They would do whatever they could to support me in attending the course. The plan was still in place.

It had been a difficult summer, with so many losses and unanswered questions about what the future held. I assured myself the program was my new beginning, the foundation stone for the rest of my life. There would be no going backward—only forward. My group therapist from the course had different ideas.

The concept of group therapy was new to me, and as the first day approached, my feelings of excitement turned into nervousness. On the first day of classes, I was self-conscious about my appearance and condition. I was tired and bloated from the cocktail of drugs that had been injected into my bruised left arm the previous week. I wore a bright, colorful scarf to cover my bald head and long, silver earrings to distract attention from the dark circles under my eyes that the makeup could not conceal. There were eight people in my group as well as the stern-faced, male group therapist. Everyone was sitting cross-legged in a circle when I entered the room. There was one priest, one former nun, a guy around my age, and the rest were women in their fifties. We started the eight-hours-long session by going around the circle and introducing ourselves. It turned out that everyone had participated in some form of group therapy in the past. They had all done the foundation year required by the institute to enroll in the course, and many of them knew each other. They looked and sounded like they knew how it worked.

In my haste to get started with my plan, I had applied directly for a place on the professional course. In my interview, I explained that my life experience of dealing with cancer in my twenties and the personal therapy I had been attending for the past year were equivalent to a foundation year. I was desperate to get a place; the next part-time course didn't start for another two years, and I didn't want to wait. Luckily, my interviewers agreed and the acceptance letter arrived in the post. So there I was, five months later, in the corner of the room, propped up against the wall with oversized pillows, trying not to look too sick or too tired, in case the group therapist thought I wasn't well enough to be there. I listened as, one by one, people started to speak about why they were there, their experiences of counseling and therapy, and what they wanted to work on.

One woman spoke at great length about how furious she was at her father, who had been dead for twenty years. She started getting really angry, shouting and cursing at the ceiling. Another person spoke so quietly I could hardly hear her; she wanted to connect with her inner voice and power. Someone else shouted, cried, and punched a cushion all the way through her introduction, which included something about a neglected inner child. By the end of the morning session, I thought, These people are nuts! I have nothing in common with any of them, and I have already paid and signed up for this for three years. Shit! I was unnerved by how open, vulnerable, and expressive everyone was, and it was only the first day. I was also shocked at myself, for being so judgmental. By the afternoon, I could feel my judgment turning into anger. I thought, I have cancer, I am fighting for my life, and I am sitting here listening to all your petty issues. Get over it people!

I was the last one to speak. By the time it was my turn, I had put every ounce of energy I had into staying awake and keeping myself together. I carefully rehearsed my introduction in my head several times. I told them, in a very matter-of-fact tone, that I discovered I had a third occurrence of breast cancer the day after I was accepted to the course, and that I wanted to use this experience to help me move forward in my life. I was not going to waste my time sitting around moaning about the past. I just wanted to change my career. That's why I was there. There was no way I was going to start digging up my past and blaming my parents for everything, like some American television show. I liked *Oprah*— but that was not what I signed up for.

They all just looked at me blankly, like they knew something I didn't. I thought I saw a smile creep onto the group therapist's face. The idea of being a therapist appealed to me, but I was quickly discovering that the group process did not. I liked the therapeutic process in the comfort and safety of my personal therapy sessions with Freda, where I felt safe and protected; I had control over what I wanted to talk about and how far I was willing to go. In the group, I had no control over what was up for discussion and felt catapulted out of my comfort zone. My journey of self-discovery got off to a rough start.

Those first few months of the course were exhausting for me. In addition to weekly personal therapy and prolonged hours of group therapy, there were lectures to attend, books to read, and papers to write. I was "therapied out" and needed a break. Hesitantly, I signed up for one week at a residential holistic recovery center, called Slánú, in the west of Ireland. It was a four-hour drive from Dublin, so I offered my cousin, Tommy, a lift as far as Galway City, where he attended university. I was glad he was in the car, as it took my mind off where I was going. Tommy was a real music buff, and we passed the long drive comparing our knowledge of obscure indie bands. As long as Larry Gogan, Ireland's oldest daytime disc jockey, wasn't playing it on the "Top 40 Hits Show," it was up for discussion. About twenty minutes outside of Galway, there was a lull in the music conversation, and Tommy asked, "So cuz, what's this place that you are going to all about?" I had avoided talking about it for the entire journey. Every time I thought about where I was going during the drive, I felt sick to my stomach. Tommy seemed to be genuinely interested and waited for my response. There was a long gap as I considered how to respond to his straightforward question. I did not like gaps and was frantically searching for a response. What was this place I was going to, anyway? I decided to go for the jovial, sarcastic response, which would still give me some credibility as the "out there," full-of-life, and fun cousin who had similar music tastes to her younger, music-mad cousin. "Oh, it's one of those holistic health places, you know: mind, body, spirit. They offer lots of different alternative therapies, vegetarian food, that kind of stuff. It's probably run by a bunch of hippies, you know the deal. I thought I'd check it out for fun and see what it's all about."

"Sounds cool," was his only response, as he turned up the car stereo, which blasted "Hey There Lonely Girl." I wondered if it was a sign: maybe that was where I was really going, to a place full of lonely girls. About an hour after I dropped off Tommy, I pulled into a gas station. I was lost. I had just entered the Gaeltacht, a remote part of the country where the Irish language is still spoken and all the road signs are in Gaelic. I knew it couldn't be too far away, as I was in the small coastal village where the venue was located. The old lady behind the counter had one eye on me and one eye on the television, which was blaring an old episode of *Dallas* in Irish. J. R. Ewing speaking Irish looked and sounded quite bizarre. As soon as I asked her for directions, I could have sworn her look changed from suspicion to sympathy in an instant. "Oh, is that what brought you here? It's just around that bend, beyond the big gates. It's the old convent building. May God be with you. Good luck."

"Thanks a million!" I cheerfully called out, as I took the yogurt-covered raisins and pack of trail mix I bought and stuffed them in my pocket, in case the vegetarian food wasn't enough.

I got into my car and shouted out loud, "What the f★★★?" Then the internal dialogue started. A convent? What the hell was she talking about? Nobody on the phone mentioned a convent. Jesus Christ. Another fine mess I had gotten myself into. If I had known that before, there was no way I would have come. And what was that look about? What was she looking at me like that for? Was she feeling sorry for me because she assumed she knew why I was going to that place? What the hell did she know anyway? She knew nothing about me or why I was going there, so piss off with your pathetic, "God bless you, good luck!" I was furious. As far as I was concerned, she might as well have said,

"Good luck, you poor pitiful fool looking for miracles, you're doomed" In my mind, that is what she did say.

It's funny how we can interpret comments made by complete strangers. When I was nine or ten, I remember a man saying to my father in Gaelic Park, where my sister and I were competing in an Irish dancing competition, "You have two fine girls there, Liam." Years later, my sister and I talked about it, and it turned out we both heard, "You have two big fatsoes for daughters, Liam." It wasn't true, but that is what we both heard. So I had a history of listening with a self-critical ear when I was feeling small and vulnerable. Really, I knew the old lady was being kind. I wasn't being kind to myself, as usual. I felt alone, scared, and nervous. I drove around the bend and sat in the car outside the convent gates. I had finally arrived at Slánú. It had been a long road, full of twists and turns, to finally get there.

I had seen the advertisement for Slánú a few months previously in the hospital, while I was having a chemotherapy treatment. The colorful rainbow on the poster made me smile. Slánú was a retreat center for people dealing with a cancer diagnosis. As far as I knew, it was the only place in Ireland that took a holistic approach to cancer. They were all about promoting harmony and balance in body, mind, and spirit, offering complementary therapies, art, vegetarian food, and information on nutrition. It sounded wonderful and exactly what I was looking for, even if I was a little skeptical. I took down the number and phoned to check it out.

The woman on the other end of the phone sounded normal enough and promised to send me some literature about the weeklong retreat program. I received the brochure, read it, and put it away in the kitchen drawer for a couple of weeks, but I couldn't stop thinking about it. I wanted a break and a rest, yet I wasn't sure I wanted to go someplace where everyone had cancer.

I came up with several reasons why I couldn't go. First of all, I couldn't afford it (though it wasn't very expensive). Subsequently, my friends raised the money. Second, the dates of the next scheduled retreat in November clashed with my chemotherapy. Later I received a phone call to say they had to reschedule the original dates, due to an unforeseen circumstance. The new dates fit in perfectly with my chemotherapy schedule. It was clear to me that the Universe was conspiring to get me there. So I packed my bag, drove across the country, and sat outside the convent gates, wondering what I had gotten myself into.

November in Ireland is a far cry from the romantic and idyllic picture postcards you see of rolling, green fields and people sitting outside pubs, clinking pints of Guinness. It is dark, wet, and wild. For seven days there would be no phone and no email or television in the back o' beyond of the Gaeltacht. It was what I kept saying I wanted, and yet I had so much resistance to being in a place where I could slow down and be quiet, away from everyone who knew me.

That first evening, I joined the group by sitting in one of the thirteen hard-backed chairs that were set in a circle. As soon as I saw the chairs, I thought, Oh no, not another group circle! There were all shapes and sizes occupying the chairs and looking around the room. I was definitely the youngest, and there was only one man. How was I going to spend a week here with these people, and what the hell would I have in common with any of them? Oh, yeah: cancer. Everyone had cancer in common, and that made me feel the most uncomfortable. I did not want to identify with a group of people who had cancer.

When it was my turn to speak, I would be ready; I had my protective persona and accouterments all in place. It had changed from the dark work suit to a long, pink knit dress, chunky jewelry, and the fact that I had just started training as a psychotherapist.

That was the clincher, my trump card. I reckoned once the facilitators heard that, the focus would be off me, and it would be clear to everybody that I was there for my own research, to see how this particular group dynamic worked. I would just be an observer and have a good time checking out the complementary therapies, maybe have a few massages, and eat some good vegetarian food. I was tired, and I wanted a rest from all the group therapy and self-analysis stuff. I was there to get away from all that. Waiting in my chair, I was able to boil it down to a couple of sentences.

The facilitator introduced herself and proceeded to ask us to respect each other's space. If someone started to cry or get upset, we should resist the urge to run over and console them. Even if it seemed heartless, we should just back off and let the person be upset. We went around the circle, and everyone genuinely seemed very nice. It was a little kumbayah-ish, but not too bad. Still, it didn't mean I had to spill my guts or even have much to do with any of them. I would stick to the plan and use this time as a little vacation for myself. I kept saying this over and over to myself, not really listening to what the others were saying, when suddenly it was my turn.

I started my prepared introduction, and before I had finished my first sentence, I could hear my voice breaking up. Tears started to well and fall, and I had just started speaking. What was happening? Everyone sat still looking at me. I wanted to run and hide, but I couldn't move or speak. All I could do was cry. I was crying in front of a group of complete strangers, and I was not even supposed to be there. I was not supposed to be in a circle with a bunch of people who had cancer!

I don't know how long I sat there, crying my way through my introduction. Crying in front of people was a big no-no for me. It was an unspoken agreement at home that no one cried in front anyone else. God forbid I let myself cry in front of my family; it would be too scary for everybody else and vice versa. So we always just acted like it was all going to be okay. Nobody needed to be dramatic and show how terrified we all really were. What good would that do? Better to keep it all bottled up inside and explode in front a group of complete strangers who were all just as terrified themselves.

Nobody said anything and nobody ran over to hug me, which was a huge relief: it was okay to cry. That was how the week began. I only stayed because I kept telling myself I could leave. I am glad I stayed, as that week was the turning point for me in accepting that I did have cancer and that everything *wasn't* okay. One of the first exercises we were asked to do was to choose a partner, sit opposite each other in silence, and look into each other's eyes for ten minutes. Here we go, I thought. I cringed and knew there was no way I would be able to keep a straight face. My partner's name was Julia She was about sixty years old, with short flaming red hair, large glasses, and a long turquoise shawl that was thrown carefully over her shoulders. I knew she was totally into it when she did not respond to my smirks implying what a crock of shit the whole thing was. She sat straight-faced opposite me, for what seemed like the longest ten minutes of my life. When it was over, we were invited to share with one another what it was like.

I lied, smiled, and said it was a pleasant experience. Close to tears, Julia continued to gaze deeply into my eyes and said she could see a deep and profound sadness in me, and she wondered how could this have happened to such a beautiful young woman? The depth of emotion and the sincerity of her response jolted me. No one had ever said anything like that to me before. Up until then, everyone kept on telling me how great I was coping, how great I looked, and how great it would be when I could put this whole thing behind me and get back to normal. My mom had a wonderful way of being eternally optimistic. Not one to put a damper on things, her reports on my well-being ranged from how fantastic to how absolutely fantastic I was doing with the whole cancer thing. I had so much resistance to admitting feeling sad about it and letting anyone else in on my sadness. I thought I had done a pretty good job being creative and positive and protecting myself and everyone else from the sadness I felt inside. It was as if Julia had gazed through one of my many layers of denial. She expressed and mirrored back the grief that I could not.

It turned out Julia was the official "observer" on the retreat that week. She was a therapist, training to be a leader on the next retreat. She was also a ten-year breast cancer survivor, specializing in imagery work. Later that evening, she offered to do some imagery work with me. I accepted her invitation, even though I didn't know what it was. Julia led me on a guided meditation, during which I clearly saw myself carrying a heavy bag on my back. I told her it felt like it was full of bricks. She invited me to put it down and look inside. When I put the bag down and opened it, I realized it was my life. I was overcome with sadness. It was a bag full of heavy labels, identities, self-judgments, and self-doubts. Initially, I was horrified to see what I had been carrying around for so long. It felt overwhelming to see my life compared to a heavy bag of bricks. Then I thought of all the energy and effort I had put into carrying around that bag. If I put as much energy and effort into putting it down, maybe my life and my journey could change course.

As the retreat progressed, emotions started to run high during some of the group discussions. People were openly sharing their hopes and fears around cancer. I stayed quiet for most of the sessions. Then, during the middle of the retreat, Peter, the only man in the group, who was there from London, grieving his sister who had died from breast cancer during the year, pointed his finger at me and shouted, "You! You think you are so together—you're not.

You are so protected, no one can get near you!" I froze. I did not see that coming nor did I see myself that way. I saw myself as open minded and fun loving. What was he talking about? I immediately got defensive and drew further into myself. I hated confrontation, and I especially hated having my cover blown.

Suddenly, sitting there in the circle, I finally realized how much I had been hiding from myself and everyone else. My heart and my soul "got it" for the first time that week, and all I could do was cry. Cry for myself, for the girl sitting in the hard-backed chair. I thought I had outsmarted it. I had made some changes; I always looked on the bright side; I never let it get me down; I kept going, kept moving, more ambitious than ever. I had just started training as a psychotherapist, for Christ's sake! I was crouched over in the chair, crying for the girl who thought she had done a good job. It finally sank in: I could not continue living the way I had up until that moment, and yet I didn't know another way to live. I covered my face with both of my hands, bent over, and sobbed, rocking back and forth, hunched over. The tears and snots flowed like a river, and I had no idea when or how they would ever stop.

I realized I was so ashamed of getting cancer again. I cried for the rest of the week. My body ached from crying so much. I had always been afraid to break down and cry. My therapist often asked me what was the worst thing that could happen if I started crying. My reply was always the same: I was afraid I wouldn't be able to stop. Well my fear had been met that week, and I had survived it. I was still in Slánú and to my surprise, everyone else survived my crying too.

That week in Slánú opened floodgates of sadness for me. It also opened me up to a healing process that would deeply enrich my life. I discovered that my resistance to feeling the sadness had caused me more pain than the actual experience of it.

When I arrived at Slánú, I thought I felt tired from all the self-analysis, chemotherapy, and unanswered questions spinning around in my head, but that week I realized I was exhausted from resisting and avoiding taking an honest look at how empty my life felt and from pushing away the questions and answers that made me nervous. I was right to feel nervous, because I was questioning the very foundations I had built my life upon. I felt the weight of the world on my shoulders, and by the end of the week, I realized it wasn't the weight of the world, it was the weight of the *shoulds*, *if onlys*, and *not enoughs* that I had been toting around like a bag of bricks. It was the weight of carrying the labels and identities that felt soulless to me. I was devastated. What had I been doing with my life? That week, I looked into the heavy bag and placed each "brick" outside of myself, and I knew if I wanted to live a full and amazing life as my true self, I could not support my habits and my old life any longer.

But instead of feeling lighter, I felt empty. What was it all for? I had no partner, no children, and no great career that I believed in or loved. I didn't have a particularly strong faith, either. Sure, I always said a few *Hail Marys* on airplanes, when turbulence kicked in, and I often made bargains with God—if so and so happened, I would do such and such—that was about the depth of it. I asked for help, and when things went the way I wanted them to, I believed, and then quickly forgot about it. Well, nothing was going the way I thought it was supposed to, and I had no idea what living a full and amazing life as my true self even looked like. I didn't know who my true self was. That week, I clearly saw what it wasn't. As hard and upsetting as it was, I knew there was no going back to carrying around what no longer served me or who I wanted to become.

On the last day of the retreat, affirmation cards were placed face down in a circle, and I pulled: "My authentic self is powerful, loving, and unafraid." I left Slánú with that card in my pocket, determined to believe it and live my way into it. I couldn't go back to pretending everything was okay, and I didn't know how to move forward, so I stayed and rested in that dark, uncomfortable place for several months. It felt as if the tears had broken up a belief system that I had outgrown. I hoped the tears would bring me some place true.

I spent that winter moving between the couch and the psychotherapy course, not knowing what else to do. It was February, and I still had not been back to work. It had already been eight months since my "end of the world" diagnosis, when it had been clear to me: stop or you will die. But I was getting nervous about how long I had been missing from the office. I had already been off for six months, enough time for a financial reality check to kick in. What would I do for money if I did not go back?

I was taking part in the psychotherapy training, but it would be years before I could call myself a therapist, and I was not even sure I wanted to spend my life listening to other people's problems. It was bad enough sitting in group therapy sessions listening to my fellow classmates work out their personal issues. I wasn't sure if I had the patience to listen anymore. Just get over it! I often thought to myself. Really, I was running out of patience with myself. As each month passed by, I set a new deadline for when I would return. That is exactly what it was, a *dead*line. There was no life or inkling of joy in setting any of those dates. Pick a day to return to what you promised yourself you would never do again. I felt conflicted. How could I go back to being a claims adjuster in a reinsurance company and remain true to the feelings and discoveries I was making about my life and myself? On the other hand, my employers had been so patient and understanding, paying me my full salary the entire time I was off. I felt obligated, by guilt, to go back. There I was battling with myself all over again. Go

back, don't go back, go back, don't go back. Of all the bricks in
the bag at Slánú, my job felt the heaviest to me, and as much as I
wanted to put it down completely, I was not able to fully let it go
at that point. I talked it over with my mom, who suggested I wait
until I finished chemo and then have a conversation with my boss
about returning on a part-time basis. No one had ever worked
there part-time before, so I assumed it was not an option. Luckily,
I had just finished reading *The Four Agreements* by Don Miguel
Ruiz, and one of the four is: "Don't assume anything." So I asked
my boss, I waited, and the response came back, "Yes, let's try it."

I went back to work on a part-time basis in April, after I finished all my chemotherapy. I brought Peggy with me this time.
I ditched the power suits and dressed in more colorful clothes,
mixing in a little bit of my bohemian spirit but not too much,
so I could get away with it. I wore my chunky silver jewelry
and big rings. I left the briefcase at home and left work on time.
After a few weeks, though, I noticed myself slipping into my old
habits. I started working a little later every day and accepting the
invitations to go out drinking after work. I didn't care about the
claims files sitting on my desk or the budgets that were waiting
to be balanced. I began to wonder: what was the point of all the
work I was doing on myself and trying to beat cancer, if I had to
do this for the rest of my life? It all seemed so meaningless to me.

Two months later, my doctor signed me off work for three
weeks for depression. He told me I needed to get a grip, pull
myself together, and just get on with it. In a group therapy session
a few days later, with the help of my group therapist, I realized
the doctor did not tell me that—I told it to myself, in a harsh and
demanding voice. "Get a grip and get on with it, for God's sake.
You're fine!" It was the same thing I had told myself after the car
accident, the abortion (which I never told the group about), and
each cancer diagnosis.

I never liked taking up too much time in group therapy to talk about myself or process a feeling, especially when I had no idea where it came from or where it would lead. At the time, I thought that was because I was sensitive to the other people in the group, and that I wanted them each to have enough time to work on their issues. Theirs always seemed more important and pressing than mine did. I reasoned it would have been selfish of me to take up too much time. Also, I didn't want any special treatment just because I had cancer. So most of the time, I just listened and spoke to give feedback. It was much easier to believe that I was being generous and was silent for selfless reasons, as opposed to being too afraid to risk taking the time and space for myself, to explore the unknown territory of my heart and soul.

Over the months, I learned the skills of empathic listening (without judging too much) and was often startled by the amount of anger and grief that came out of group members during sessions. Pillows were pounded, expletives were emphatically shouted into the circle or at the group therapist, and I could have sworn that our group alone kept Kleenex in business, with all the crying that went on. All the time I listened, I noticed how uncomfortable I felt in my body every time someone expressed anger that felt out of control to me. I was okay with the crying, and often felt great compassion for my classmates, but I couldn't bear the anger. My breathing would get shallow, and I could feel my chest start to tighten every time. I wanted it to stop. Now I know it was because I could not bear to look at or feel my own anger.

Anger was never openly expressed in a healthy way when I was growing up, so I always assumed it was bad and best kept under wraps. I only remember my father ever getting really angry on a couple of occasions, and my mother putting it out as quickly as it arose. The unspoken message I picked up was: it is not okay to express anger, frustration, or disappointment. There was so much to be grateful for, after all; why get mad? So instead of getting angry, I got in a "bad mood" and retreated to my bedroom. When I was a kid and teenager, it was much more acceptable to be moody than angry. Now I wasn't moody, I was depressed. Or was I? My group therapist didn't seem to think so. He suggested, from his observations over the months, that the heaviness I was feeling could actually be repressed anger that I was not expressing. He suggested I try to move toward the anger and connect with it, instead of pushing it down. What the hell was he talking about? I had no idea how he came up with that one. I felt lost and confused. Me? Angry? I thought I was the least dramatic, the most fun-loving, and optimistic one in the group. What did he know anyway? He only saw me for a few hours every month. Wasn't it okay for me to just be depressed for a while? I left the group that day feeling angry with him for suggesting such a thing. In any case, even if it was true, I had no idea how to "move toward it" and "connect with it." I didn't get angry.

A few days later I was listening to a new CD at home that a friend made for me, and a song by the Icelandic artist Bjork came on, which I had never heard before, called "Hyperballad." It started off slow and melodic, telling a story of a woman standing on the top of a mountain throwing things off—like auto parts, knives, forks, and anything else she found lying around the place—and then the rhythm gradually started building into a techno-electronic dance beat. The story progressed to her imagining what her body would look like falling against the rocks, even wondering if her eyes would be open when she hit the ground. She performed this ritual alone every morning in silence, while her lover slept, so she could be "happy" to be with him when he woke up. The tempo continued climbing and climbing, until she finally kept repeating, "say nothing," as if she were in a trance. Before I had time to think about it, I jumped up and started dancing to the intense beat that filled the room, all the time mouthing the words, "say nothing," over and over again. The intensity of the music, the words, the images, and the beat awakened something inside me that I couldn't speak about. Yet I could feel it and move with it. It felt like bottled up anger and frustration.

The song then started moving through me, and I was transformed into a whirling dervish in the middle of the living room—within three minutes. I felt exhilarated by the energy and continued playing the song over and over again until I collapsed onto the couch, completely exhausted. Somehow, hearing the story of the song, along with the rising techno beat and the repetition of "say nothing," awakened feelings that I had no words for, but it felt like something wanted to come out. For days, I played the song continuously, in an attempt to dance the feelings out of my body.

At the next group therapy session, I risked sharing my whirling dervish dance experience with the group. The therapist asked me, "What if you could say something? What would it sound like?"

I closed my eyes, thought of the music, got to my feet, and to my great surprise, started shouting at the top of my lungs: "It's not fair!" "I'm too young!" "I hate this!" "Fuck this!" "I don't want this!" I looked around the circle, slightly embarrassed, quickly scanning group members' faces for criticism—there wasn't any.

"What else?" the therapist calmly asked. "Is there more? It's safe to go there now. We are all here for you. It's okay, just let it go." I had permission.

Suddenly, out of nowhere, I saw myself trapped in the car wreck ten years earlier. I howled and shouted like I never had before, cursing the drunk driver for crashing into us, furious that I was even there in the first place. I didn't want to go out that night! I didn't want my friend to die! I didn't want to pretend anymore that it wasn't that bad! I didn't want to have to look at the scar on my face for the rest of my life! But I would have to, and it made me furious. Then, in my mind, I saw the long jagged scar across my chest, instead of my breast, and I roared from some place deep in the bottom of my belly that I never knew existed. I was shocked by the excruciating sounds I made, but I couldn't stop and I didn't want to. I screamed for having my bald head shoved down a toilet bowl, throwing up for hours after having chemo, and for feeling trapped in a life and a career that I didn't want anymore. Raw and primal anger rose up from inside me, and it kept coming. There was so much more that I couldn't explain or figure out, and for the first time in my life, I didn't try to hide it or disguise it as something else—I let it loose. I punched pillows, threw myself on the ground, screamed and howled like a wild banshee, for what seemed like an eternity. When it felt like there was nothing left to come out, I lay down on the cushions I had punched earlier, and the whole group sat in a circle around me, saying nothing, holding the space. A great silence filled the room. It felt sacred.

To my great relief, I survived the outburst of anger that had been building up for years, and so did everybody else. Just like everybody in the group at Slánú had survived my tears a few months earlier. My body was exhausted, I couldn't move, but my heart felt huge, as if it had burst wide open. A dark cloud had lifted from my chest, and energy pulsated through my body that was alive, exhilarating, and new. I imagined that was how it would have felt if I had just given birth. In way, I had.

That day, in the safety of the group circle, I gave birth to a part of myself that I didn't know existed. It was the part that had been buried underneath "saying nothing" and "getting on with it"; the part that was outraged at the injustices of life and was full of hurt and anger. It was a ferocious part of me that needed to have a voice, be honored, heard, witnessed, and brought to life.

Now that I was aware it existed, I could no longer ignore it, and I didn't want to. It was too big, and I realized it held an enormous amount of power and energy. I had lost a lot of personal power by putting so much energy into pushing my anger and disappointment down, into the dark regions of my body and psyche, out of sight and hearing, where it festered and grew. It was time to turn toward it, listen to it, and relate to it, so I could harness its incredible force to help give me the strength to move in the direction of my heart, instead of using it to fuel my old struggles.

After that experience, I stopped telling myself, "just get on with it." Get on with what, anyway—pushing down my anger, so I wouldn't piss off anybody? Or keeping a job that felt like I was living half a life? Connecting with my anger helped me come to the realization: there was no way I could continue to "say nothing" because I didn't want to rock the boat or because I was afraid of not knowing what would happen next. For the previous six months, I had worked hard trying to let go of my tight grip on what I thought I was "supposed to be doing" and how I was "supposed to be living." I knew I couldn't go back to working, or living, part time. I decided to quit. I had nothing lined up, a meager savings, with two years left on the course before there was even a possibility of earning any money. I didn't care; I was ready to let go—it was time.

The same morning I planned to tell my boss, he called me into his office. He had something to tell me. He was sorry, but it was obvious it was not working out. The company offered to put me on professional disability. They would claim me as a liability on their insurance policy and pay me two thirds of my salary for five years. I could hardly believe my ears. I felt as if he handed me the get-out-of-jail-free card! I left the office for good that day, almost a year to the day I had left on my lunch break to go to the breast clinic. I never went back again.

Somehow, I connected this amazing luck or grace to what I learned at Slánú. *Slánú* is an Irish word that means, "being saved or being led into the fullness of life." My time there was the beginning of my path toward fullness. I didn't know how to get there by myself. I had so much resistance to going in the first place; I guess there was something inside of me that knew it would change me forever. In any case, something bigger than myself led me there. During my time at Slánú, I realized how self-protected I was, thinking I had to know how things were going to go and being unwilling to take risks. Slánú also prepared me for entering into a relationship with my shadow, a powerful part of me that contributes to the fullness of my being. It was a pivotal point in terms of my personal journey and my career. I finally understood that they went hand in hand.

Could it be that cancer was not a detour on that journey? Maybe cancer was life itself calling out to me to have a sense of adventure, to take more and more risks, and to open more fully to life. I sensed it was time for me to stop, listen, and start living my life in search of what really mattered. I still didn't have any big answers to my big questions, but I took the advice of Rilke, "Live the questions now. Perhaps, then, someday far in the future, you will gradually, without even noticing it, live your way into the answer." I would finally let myself step into the unknown and participate in it instead of pushing it away. That was it: I would start living the questions.

8

Blossoming into Life

*May your life be like a wildflower, growing freely in
the beauty and joy of each day.*

—AMERICAN INDIAN PROVERB

After having spent the last year in and out of the hospital,
receiving chemo, recovering from chemo, plotting, schem-
ing, and worrying over how I would leave work and start my
new life–it was all over. I was free at last! As delighted as I was to
be finished going to the hospital, there was a safety and security
I felt from being monitored so closely. The euphoria and excitement of finishing treatment soon changed to fear. How would I
know if it was coming back? New precautions were set in place.
The appointments changed to every three months. I would take
a drug called tamoxifen every day for five years, to suppress the
release of estrogen, as my tumor was estrogen positive. My periods would stop while I was on it; they might not ever resume.
Early menopause might set in; they didn't know. I was assured this
was good news. It would help reduce the chances of recurrence.

For the whole year, I was being taken care of by doctors,
nurses, friends, concerned workmates and classmates—not to
mention my parents, whose couch I had claimed as my second
bedroom. Chemo was over, work was over, and the psychother-

apy course was over for the summer. Now what? I couldn't hide out at my parents' house forever, nor did I want to. I wanted to get as far away from the cancer and therapy worlds as possible. I wanted an adventure. On the next visit to my oncologist, I told him of my longing to travel and asked if there was any place I should avoid. "Iran and Iraq," was his deadpan response. It was clear that it was time to stop being so nervous about everything and go have some fun!

But where to go? I first considered going to Indonesia, lured by the white, sandy beaches, warm water, sunshine, and its exotic and magical culture. It sounded like paradise. Then, later that week, I heard on the news that civil war had just broken out there. Paradise would have to wait; I had enough war waging within myself. I wanted to go somewhere far away that felt safe and healing. In a therapy session, Freda suggested we do a guided meditation and ask for the place to be revealed to me. A few years previously, that would have sounded like a crazy idea to me, but not now.

During all my chemotherapy, I had also been receiving regular Reiki treatments, which I believed helped me to recover from the chemo and opened me to the energy and the healing capacity of my body in a new way. I had some incredible experiences that my rational brain could not explain. Sometimes I could see colors and sense guides around me, so it wasn't such a crazy concept to me to ask for guidance in a meditation.

Freda led the thirty-minute meditation. When it was over, I knew where I wanted to go: Arizona. I had been there ten years previously, when I was living in New York. A girlfriend and I went for five days on vacation. We hiked the Grand Canyon, totally unprepared, with no water, hat, or sunscreen. We were naïve twenty-one-year-olds living in the Bronx, removed from and unconscious of the power of nature and the elements. I will never forget my friend stopping about fifteen minutes from the top, sunburned and thirsty, crying out, "This is the cruelest thing I have ever done to myself!"

That is where I wanted to go. In the meditation, I saw a clear, blue, expansive sky and huge red cliffs. I also heard drumming that sounded Native American (although it was probably the tape Freda was playing). It didn't matter, I was convinced it was Arizona and declared that was where I would go. As soon as I got home, I phoned my cousin Marie in London, who also happened to be my best friend. I wanted her to come with me and hoped she would be able to. I knew she loved to travel. She was working as a contract nurse, making good money, and had a flexible schedule, meaning she could take off as much time as she wanted. She thought about it and called me back the next day. Thelma and Louise eat your heart out—Arizona here we come!

Three weeks later, we arrived in Phoenix. The only research either of us had done was to purchase a *Lonely Planet* guidebook at Heathrow airport. I was sick and tired of having plans. We agreed it would be a real adventure, without an itinerary. The first stop was Hertz Rent-A-Car. All good adventures required wheels. Marie used her lovely English accent to negotiate a good deal on renting an unadventurous-looking Ford for six weeks. The excitement started when we maneuvered out of the car rental garage and onto the highway. Neither of us had ever driven in the States before. We were used to driving stick shifts—on the opposite side of the road. We eventually found a Super 8 motel off the highway, when we were finally brave enough to take an exit ramp. We decided to make our way to Sedona the following morning.

Sedona is a spectacular place located about 4,500 feet above sea level, with huge red rocks bursting into the skyline that look like they are glowing at sunrise and sunset. I passed through it briefly ten years previously, and even though I had never heard of the words *chakra* or *vortex* back then, I still felt it was a very special place. I always referred to it fondly as Fred Flintstone country. Sedona is renowned for being a New Age center. It's a mecca that attracts spiritual seekers from all around the world. It is also popular with sports enthusiasts, due to the miles and miles of hiking and biking trails throughout the breathtaking terrain. Marie and I did not fall under the sporting or New Age enthusiasts categories, but I was certainly curious.

We spent the first few days by the Super 8 motel pool, adapting to our new environment. It was dramatically different from Ireland in every way one could imagine. The predominant color of the landscape was red instead of green, and the sun never seemed to stop shining. July temperatures soared over one hundred degrees, and there was no humidity; stepping out of an air-conditioned room was like stepping into an oven. The sunshine and the red earth and cliffs made my heart sing—it was heaven to me.

I couldn't wait to go exploring. The town had changed significantly from what I remembered. It seemed everywhere you turned, there was another crystal shop. In almost every store and restaurant we went into, the assistant or server was either an artist, healer, or psychic. All worked part-time to earn their bread and butter, so they could afford to do what they loved. They usually slipped us their card on our way out the door.

I could understand why they were all lured there. The place had a magical quality to it, and the scenery was mind blowing. Everyone we met looked happy and healthy. It was no wonder, as there were fantastic health food stores and supermarkets catering to the health-conscious mountain bikers and hikers that we passed in our air-conditioned car every day. I looked at them through the car window and thought I wanted to do that too someday. Another day, we drove down a one-way street—the wrong way. The guy in the car approaching us reversed all the way back down the street so we could pass. We apologized and thanked him profusely. He simply smiled, waved, and called out, "Not a biggie!" That became our motto for the rest of the trip. Nothing was a biggie. I still say it to myself all the time.

One day while visiting one of the town's many art galleries, a series of paintings caught my eye. During the previous year, I had been given a beautiful card that had a strong and fearless-looking Native American woman on it, in full, colorful headdress, wearing a turquoise choker and earrings. Her long black hair was flowing in the wind. Behind her were snowcapped mountains and underneath her, a pack of wolves were running across a desert. I loved that card, so I framed it and placed it on my bedroom dresser; it had given me so much strength during the year. The paintings hanging on the walls of the gallery jumped out at me, and I wondered if it could possibly be the same artist. I casually mentioned it to the gallery owner and he said, "Oh, that's Jean's work. She lives right here in town. Let's give her a call and ask her if it's her work on the card." Before I could say anything, he started dialing her number. "Hmm, no answer. Tell you what, why don't you call her yourself." He pulled out a map of Sedona, wrote down her home number, and handed it to me with a huge smile. I thanked him and put the map in my bag. I had no intention of calling her.

When I told Marie that evening, she encouraged me to call the artist straightaway. "Things like that don't happen every day; just call her and talk to her. You have got nothing to lose. So what if she thinks you're crazy?" True, I had nothing to lose, and basically, I just wanted to let her know how much strength and encouragement I felt from her paintings.

A few days later, I called Jean from the motel. I wasn't quite sure what to say. I decided to tell her about the card I had received in Ireland, and that I thought she might be the same artist. The rest would depend on how she responded. Jean was expecting me to call, as the gallery owner gave her the heads up; it was a small town, after all. She did not remember the particular image I described but said it was possible it was one of hers. She was flattered and delighted that I took the trouble to call and introduce myself. It turned out she always wanted to visit Ireland, and she asked me loads of questions about the geography and places to visit. Eventually the topic came back to what I was doing in Sedona from Ireland. I told her about having had breast cancer and how I saw Arizona in a meditation.

The phone went silent for about ten seconds, and I wondered if we had been cut off. Then I could hear her softly crying. I immediately panicked, as her reaction surprised me. I assured her that I was fine and was having a great time in Sedona. Then she apologized and told me she had had breast cancer twelve years previously. She had dreamed of being a full-time artist her whole life but always talked herself out of it. Ten years ago, when she was in her fifties, she and her husband sold their house in the Midwest, packed up their truck, and drove to Sedona to start a new life. Life was too short not to be an artist, she reckoned. Her husband built their home and set up his construction business in town. They loved their new life, and she painted and hiked every day.

We talked for over two hours on the phone. I told her all about leaving work and having no idea what I would do or where I would live when I returned to Ireland. She shared different parts of her life, and we laughed and cried like two old friends. By the time I hung up, we had swapped addresses and promised to keep in touch. My phone call was timely, as they were leaving town the next day for Hawaii. I felt inspired and blessed to have spoken with her. She assured me anything was possible—if you were willing to risk everything.

I loved Sedona—the landscape, the people, the art, the crystals, the "energy," and I would have been happy to spend our entire time there, but I had promised Marie a road trip, and our rental car was looking sad and lonely in the Super 8 motel parking lot. We decided to hit the open road and head north. We took our time, stopping for a night here and there when we felt like it. We drove through the desert, visited Hopi and Navaho reservations, and eventually hooked up with Route 66. I loved stopping at the silver jewelry stalls on the side of the highway, and everyone seemed to have plenty of time to talk.

Marie had never seen the Grand Canyon, so we spent a few days in Flagstaff, Arizona—"Flag," as we affectionately called it by the time we left. It was a college town, so we tracked down the local brewery. There was live music every night, and they served killer pizza and beer, which tasted delicious, especially after weeks of roadside diner food and granola bars. We ate, drank, danced, and laughed our heads off for the majority of the trip. It was just what I needed.

After weeks of driving through Indian country, passing bizarre biker towns, wonders of the world, hippie communes, deserts, sophisticated Scottsdale, and hip Tucson, we headed back to Sedona for our last week. We thoroughly enjoyed our freedom and laughed our way through all our adventures around the state. However, I was relieved and excited to return to Sedona. It felt like the red rocks were welcoming us home as we drove through Oak Creek Canyon and made our way toward another motel on the other side of town.

I rented a mountain bike and cycled and hiked on some of the canyon trails, bought some books on crystals and angel cards, and did research on the phenomenal energy vortexes that were located all around the small town. The vortexes centered around four major red rock formations and were known to be places of heightened spiritual energy spiraling up from the ground. They were considered sacred sites, and people came from all around the world to visit them for prayer, meditation, and healing.

It took a few days, but I eventually talked Marie into going on a guided vortex tour with me. Our tour guide looked nothing like the picture on the flyer I saw at the local co-op. It must have been taken twenty years earlier, and she appeared a little kooky and worn out from years in the harsh sun, but she seemed to know her stuff. We, along with four other tourists, packed into her huge jeep and spent the day driving deep into the backcountry of Sedona's canyons. She told us that the spiraling energy of the vortexes connected with the inner energy of each individual; that is why we would all have different experiences. Some vortexes activated male energy, some feminine energy, and some balanced the two. Marie and I exchanged glances several times throughout the day. It all sounded a bit far-fetched, but neither of us could deny the strong presence of love and feeling of peace we felt each time we visited one of the sacred sites. That evening, our guide held a beautiful ceremony for the group at a medicine wheel, a first for me, and I set the intention to remain open to healing on all levels of my body, mind, and spirit.

Sedona awakened my old questions: Why was I here? What was it all for? But the tone of the questions had changed. The questions were infused with warmth, curiosity, and excitement to experience the answer. Sedona also awakened a sense of joy and wonder inside me, as well as a deep appreciation for the beauty that was all around me. I had just gotten a glimpse of a big, wide world, with lots of different ways to live and experience life—I was psyched. I felt like it was the beginning of leaving the ordinary world behind and entering into the next extraordinary phase of my life.

When I returned to Ireland, it felt like I had left most of my pain in the desert. Even the Irish weather could not dampen my spirits. Soon after I got back, I went to stay with my good friends, Patrick and Siobhan, who lived in Skerries, a beautiful, little coastal town on the Irish Sea, about twenty miles north of Dublin city. I had met them in London when I lived there. They moved back to Ireland around the same time I did, and they often invited me to their home for weekends. They were great fun, and they were also extremely good to me when I was sick. Siobhan and some of her friends, who barely knew me, raised the money for me to go to Slánú by organizing a dinner dance and raffle at the local sailing club. They were delighted to hear my stories of Sedona and to see me in such good form.

One evening, Siobhan and I went for a walk on the beach, and on the way back, we noticed a "For Sale by Auction" sign on one of little cottages on the street parallel to the beach. Just as we were walking past, the estate agent came out of the house. She happened to be a school friend of Siobhan's. It really was a small town; everyone seemed to know everyone and everyone else's business too! There were only two main streets, two supermarkets, one post office, three restaurants, but at least fifteen pubs. Cottages rarely came up for sale, and when they did, they were snatched up. Siobhan asked if we could see it, and as soon as we entered, she looked at me and said, "It was made for you."

I felt it too. But there was no way I could buy a house. I had just gotten signed off from work on disability. I would never get approved for a mortgage. Then I remembered: I already was approved. Two years earlier, I was searching for an apartment in Dublin city and had the mortgage papers signed by my old boss and the bank manager. Could the mortgage approval still be valid? On Monday morning, just for fun, I called my bank manager to check. It was valid as far as the bank was concerned. Oh my God, could I really consider buying a cottage by myself in a quiet fishing town outside of Dublin?

The auction was in three weeks. Sale by auction meant that when the hammer was hit, the last bidder signed the papers, wrote the down payment check, and got the keys. There was no way I could write a down payment check, I knew that for sure. I had sold my little red Ford Fiesta so I could go to Arizona for the summer. I didn't even own a car and was living paycheck to paycheck, with no savings.

I talked to my mom and dad about it, and they agreed to drive up to Skerries, about two hours from their home, to have a look. My dad had worked as a carpenter for twenty years in New York, before we moved to Ireland, so he knew what to look for when buying a house. I assured him it was very cute, and it had a great energy. Nonetheless, he said he'd see it for himself. Once my parents saw the house and the awesome location by the beach, they told me they would give me the down payment as a gift. I couldn't believe it. My parents had both worked so hard all their lives. They both went to America with nothing, worked long hours, and sent money home to their parents. My dad, with very little formal education, managed to build up a successful construction business in New York and made enough money to fulfill his dream of returning to Ireland and buying a farm. They never went on a vacation or spent money on themselves. Yet they were willing to hand me a check, so I could buy a house. And the best part was, they were so happy to do it. I was blown away by their generosity and could hardly believe how fortunate I was.

I knew what my top bid could be, based on the amount of money the bank manager had agreed to lend me two years previously. The auction would take place in Dublin city. We had no idea how many people were interested in the property or how much it would go for. My dad would do the bidding. He told my mom and me to sit in the middle of the room and pretend we did not know him. He sat in the back corner, with his overcoat and tweed peak cap tilted over his face. I wondered what all the cloak and dagger stuff was about but knew enough to not ask any question and do what I was told—for once. I had never been to an auction before. The small room was packed tight with people, but no one made a sound; tension filled the air.

The auctioneer started the bidding off at forty-five thousand pounds. You couldn't hear a sound, and then he shouted, "The gentleman in the back with the cap starts us off." And then the race was on! The speed at which the auctioneer spoke was comparable to a horseracing announcer; it was fascinating. Ears were being tugged, newspapers raised, and occasionally you would hear about the man in the back with the cap. Dad was pulling at his peak cap to mark his bid. After the furious start, the bids started slowing down. My heart was racing and pounding out of my chest. My ears were burning, and I could hear my mother whispering under her breath, "The Lord save us, Jesus, Mary, and Joseph." We were rapidly approaching what I knew was Dad's last bid.

"Going once, going twice—sold!—to the gentleman with the cap." Mom and I let out a long sigh of relief in unison and hugged each other tightly. I think we had both forgotten to breathe for the last two minutes. Then the auctioneer asked everyone to leave the room except Dad. Dad explained that I was the buyer, so Mom and I stayed too. It wasn't over yet. It turned out that the reserve price was not met. The seller expected more and wanted to withdraw it from auction. I didn't know that was allowed, but apparently it was. I knew I did not have another penny to offer, and my heart started to sink. Then my dad started talking. "Shur, it's all very well and good, expecting and wanting more; but I know meself from going to marts, selling sheep and cattle, it depends on who shows up on the day and puts the money in your hand. Please offer the seller two hundred pounds good luck money, and we'll be on our way."

The auctioneer left the three of us in the room for fifteen minutes. When he came back he said, "Your goodwill gesture was your good luck. The house is yours." I was so proud of my father.

The estate agent's literature described the cottage as "charming, compact, and bijou," which really meant: it's damn small. There was one main room that you entered from the street. It had a glass backdoor that led outside to a tiny, square-shaped patio, so there was lots of natural light, which was wonderful. There was a standing-room-only kitchen, a decent-sized bedroom, a long narrow bathroom, no closets, and an attic. That was it, and it was enough for me. I considered the long, sandy beach my backyard, as it was only a stone's throw away.

I had never owned a stick of furniture in my thirty-three years, let alone a house. I had rented furnished apartments when I lived in New York, London, and Dublin. I always thought of myself as a city person and never wanted to be tied down with a mortgage. But that was before. So much had happened in such a short time. I was willing to see myself and my life through a different lens; a much wider one, with no end to the horizon.

I had a blast decorating the cottage on a shoestring. Friends rallied round and helped me paint the walls with fabulous, vibrant yellows, pinks, and purples. We painted the wood floor in the bathroom silver, with stars on the ceiling and dolphin stencils on the side of the tub. I collected seashells from the beach and placed them on the windowsills. I hung a crystal I bought in Sedona from the kitchen window, and rainbows danced on the walls every time the sun hit it. Mom gave me an armchair from home, and I bought a twin mattress, which laid on the floor for over a year until I finally could afford the mattress frame. Oversized, colorful pillows served as a couch for several months. I invested in a Mexican pine round table and four wood chairs. Sitting around a table with friends was my favorite way to socialize. And as I didn't have much money, I figured that was where I would be doing most of my socializing.

My income dropped, but so did my expenses. I no longer had weekly dry cleaning bills or hair appointments to straighten my wild, wavy hair. I stopped going out for dinner and drinks and spending ridiculous amounts of money on work clothes. I always made sure I had enough money for essentials like candles and fresh flowers. Life was simpler. I went for long walks on the beach every day, and I bought a secondhand mountain bike. I loved riding my bike when I was a kid. Sedona had reminded me of so many simple things that brought me joy. I rode my bike for miles along the coastline most days and breathed the fresh sea air deep into my lungs, so happy to be alive.

I bought differently shaped canvases and started painting and reading books at night instead of watching television. I joined a yoga class two evenings a week and fell in love with it. It was the beginning of a love affair with life, and I was wildly in love. I wanted to keep that love alive for the rest of my days, no matter how long that might be.

Every third weekend, I attended the psychotherapy-training course on the other side of Dublin, as well as attending my weekly private therapy, which was also a requirement of the course. My relationship to all of it had changed. I wanted to take more risks in the group and go deeper into my own process. I looked forward to the course weekends and respected and grew to love my peers in the group. I was slowly becoming more conscious of my own defenses and resistances, which were the obstacles to my personal and spiritual growth. Instead of pushing them away, I got curious about them, and that made all the difference. We held a safe, strong, and loving space for each other as we all worked through our stuff. As difficult as the process was sometimes, it was also one of the most empowering and worthwhile things I have ever done.

A few months after moving to Skerries, a check arrived out of the blue, from my old employers. Apparently, I had shares in the company, and when I left, they sold them. The check was for three thousand pounds, the exact price of the bright orange 1973 VW Beetle I had my eye on. I always loved old Beetles; I thought they were so cute. I remember my father saying, "We'll see how cute it is when it breaks down on the side of the road." It wasn't so cute then, I admit. However, it was fun for a short while, and it got me in and out of town every Saturday to help at a friend's arts and crafts stall at the old Dandelion Market. I enjoyed talking to all the tourists and shoppers. I was selling fun, silly, hand-painted photo frames that had sayings on them like, "Best Friends Forever" and "Girls' Night Out." It was a far cry from what I had been working at, and it was just what I needed, light hearted, and playful! It helped at balancing all the self-reflection I was immersed in.

It took me a while to know how to respond to the questions I was often asked by people: "What do you do?" and "Are you working?" In the beginning, it quickly threw me off my center. I was never quite sure how to respond and worried what others would think of me. It felt like I was working, just in a different way. I had always been driven by doing a good job and being seen as successful. But my idea of success had changed. I no longer measured success by how much money I made. I measured success by being alive. In time, my response confidently changed to, "I am working on myself."

Life was opening up in ways I couldn't have even begun to imagine a couple of years before. The incredible thing was, I didn't plan any of it. I couldn't possibly have. It made me wonder: what else was possible?

I named the cottage *Sedona*. It was my own little healing house, far away from Arizona. It provided me with the shelter and the courage I needed to continue healing and blossoming and asking who I was becoming. It was one of the happiest times of my life, but I couldn't help wondering if I would always be alone.

CHAPTER

9

Namaste–
I Honor the Light in You

*Kindness is the light that dissolves all walls
between souls, families, and nations.*

—PARAMAHANSA YOGANANDA

There was chaos everywhere. Cars were speeding past in all directions. Cows were wandering aimlessly, one or two even stopping in the middle of the crazy traffic to take a shit. There were hundreds of people shouting and moving their heads from side to side, for no apparent reason. It looked as if people were running straight into the traffic for sport. I had to cup my hand over my nose and mouth to try and block out the intense aromas that ranged from unfamiliar spices to shit to overpoweringly sweet incense, just in case I would throw up. At the same time, a small gang of children tugged at my shirt, begging for money, which made me feel guilty, sad, and annoyed all at once. To top it off, monkeys were randomly hopping across telephone wires overhead. I wasn't dreaming. I was standing on a street corner in New Delhi, clutching Max's shirttail, wondering how in the hell we would ever get across.

I had met Max, my traveling companion, five months earlier, back in Ireland. He was visiting his mother in Skerries for the

· · · · · · · · · ·

117

summer, and we happened to be in the same Tai Chi class. My friends, Patrick and Siobhan, had mentioned him before and told me a little bit about him, so I knew his name. I had always been curious about the guy who spent the last fifteen years going to and from India, working as a fisherman during the summer and spending the rest of the year traveling in India. I introduced myself as Patrick and Siobhan's friend, and we ended up doing what most Irish people do: going to the pub after class. I explained that I had always been fascinated and intrigued by India, but especially since I had started practicing yoga earlier that year. I had lots of questions, and more than anything, I thought he was kind of cute.

Max was the most laid-back person I had ever met. Nothing seemed to faze him or get him to raise his voice above the calm, airline-pilot quality it usually exuded. He had absolutely no acquisitive interest in money or material possessions, so he didn't have much. As long as he had enough cash to live simply in India for most of the year, he was happy and content with his lot in life. I was intrigued by what might have drawn this thirty-six-year-old, conventional-looking Irish guy to go to India.

"So, Max, what enticed you to go to India in the first place?" I asked, fully expecting him to say something spiritual, like it was his great quest for truth and a burning desire to know God, or he felt he had a past life there or something. But no, it was nothing like that.

"When I was younger, I partied a lot. Then I heard that India was a cheap place to get stoned, so I tossed a few things in my backpack, and took off."

I must admit, my heart sank as all illusions of spiritual grandeur went out the window. However, he did go on to say that, after a few years of serious partying and almost dying, he realized how empty that lifestyle was. That was when he embarked on a more spiritual path of sorts. He started meditating and learning yoga;

he got interested in ayurveda, "the science of life"; and he lived very simply. Max liked his freedom and knew he never wanted to settle down or live full time in the West. He was in Dublin for the summer, and then he would be gone.

I knew straightaway he was not boyfriend material, but I liked his company, and we quickly became friends. He often knocked on my door in the middle of the afternoon, with a big smile and a bag of prawns or some kind of fresh fish that he had caught on his latest trip out to sea. After he had brought me a few bags of seafood, I told him I had no idea what to do with it. He offered to clean it and even cook it for me. He stayed for dinner, and our talks started going on later into the evenings. He would tell me wonderful tales of his travels in India, and I was always hanging on his every word. The first few nights after he went home, my girlfriends would call, wanting to know what was going on. Nothing, I assured them, we were just friends, but I noticed I was just a little too excited every time the phone rang or there was a knock on the door. I had never met anyone like him.

After two weeks, I decided that if I could not tell this totally calm, centered, and unmaterialistic man that I only had one breast, I would never be able to tell any man that I was seriously interested in. When I told him, he cried. He said he didn't care, he thought I was the most beautiful and feminine woman he had ever met, inside and out. He was interested in my heart and soul. I was quite taken aback by his reaction. I don't know what I was expecting, but it wasn't that. He went on to say that breasts were only lumps of flesh, as far as he was concerned, and they had nothing to do with the beauty that dwelled within me. I fell in love with him that night. I had not been with a man in over four years, since I was in a relationship in London. We made love that night, and I couldn't bear the thought of him leaving for India. He was like a mysterious angel that had descended into my life, always telling me how beautiful I was and how lucky he felt to know me.

We had a fantastic summer together, and I was dreading the day I knew he would leave. To my great surprise, he asked me to leave with him. As exciting as it sounded, I knew there was no way I could go; I had one more year left on the psychotherapy course, and I had just bought my house ten months ago. On the other hand, it seemed like the opportunity of a lifetime, to go to India with someone who knew it as well as Max did and who knew me and loved me for who I was. I wasn't quite sure I knew who I was myself, but maybe I could find out in India.

I started looking into it. Just because I thought of reasons why I couldn't go didn't mean I couldn't. Over the last couple of years, I had learned to question my thinking process and to stop rushing to the same old answers. First I called the institute and asked if I could take one year off the course and rejoin it the following September. The director lost her cool and said I was interrupting the program. It was not a good idea. No one had ever done it before, and they could not guarantee me a place the following year. It would depend on whether someone in the group behind me dropped out or didn't get through. I was surprised by her strong reaction and thought, wait a minute: haven't you been teaching us to trust the process all this time? This was my process, and I would trust how the cards fell. It was time to take another leap of faith—I was going.

I could get a six-month visa for India, and if I rented the house, it would cover the mortgage and then some, which could help out with traveling expenses. Contrary to my fears of the house being a ball and chain, it turned out to be a welcomed anchor; I could sail away and know that I had a safe haven to come back to. I sold my beloved orange VW Beetle and bought my ticket. India was cheap compared to Ireland, and if I was careful, I could live off the proceeds of the sale for the entire trip. It all happened so fast that before I knew it, I was standing on a New Delhi street corner hanging on to Max for dear life.

Nothing could have prepared me for India. It truly was a culture shock. At home, it felt like anything was possible, and in India, it felt like anything could happen! Nothing was easy. The most helpful thing Max said to me, before we left, was to forget the idea of having personal space—something that was important to me and most Westerners, and is totally alien to Indians. I remember getting on my first bus in the Himalayas. Since there wasn't an available seat, I suggested we wait for the next bus, which might not be so crowded, so we could sit together for the twelve-hour drive across the mountains. Max just laughed and said the next bus might not be for days, and this one wasn't crowded—yet. I watched dumbfounded as at least sixty more people crammed into the bus, and another twenty or thirty climbed out of the windows to sit and hang off the roof.

Traveling was a death-defying act in itself. It appeared that the only way to let another vehicle know you were coming around a hairpin turn, on a steep mountainside, was to honk your horn. From what I could gather, whoever went the fastest and honked the loudest went first. On every single journey, we passed horrific crashes along the roadside. Death never seemed very far away.

On the other hand, the whole country was exploding with life. Life was everywhere. In the cities, Bollywood music blared from each bus, rickshaw, and vendor cart that lined the streets. Anywhere we went, we encountered a restless sea full of color, sounds, and smells. People, animals, and vehicles occupied every inch of space in what I can only describe as total and utter organized chaos. All of our senses were on high alert because we needed them all—to stay alive! It was terrifying and exciting to take one step off the edge of the curb and get caught up in the energetic web that was keeping the whole thing moving and together at the same time. It felt dangerous and exhilarating all at once.

I loved it and hated it. There was never an in-between feeling for one moment of the entire six months I was there. I was blasted out of my comfort zone the moment I arrived, and I deeply understood that I knew *nothing*, not even how to go to the bathroom or eat. I had heard about the absence of toilet paper, so I brought my own, which ran out after a few days, due to an early onslaught of "Delhi-belly." Eating anything with your left hand was a major faux pas, again because of the lack of toilet paper, if you know what I mean.

Our first stop was a tiny village at the foothills of the Himalayas. Max had been going there by himself for nearly ten years. He always rented the same house, which was about a forty-minute hike from the village, straight up. It took longer with a heavy rucksack on your back. The only way to get there was to walk, as there was no road. He assured me it was worth the effort, that the house was really special. The "house" was a log cabin on wooden stilts, which had stacks of cut firewood underneath it. There was a twelve-foot ladder leaning against it that led to the front door. This immediately freaked me out, because I was afraid of heights. I hated climbing ladders, especially rickety ones, but that was the only way to access the cabin. Inside the one and only room, a thin mattress was thrown in the corner. There was a wood-burning stove in the middle of the floor and some shelves with a few cups, plates, and half-empty spice bottles scattered around. The house stood alone on the side of the mountain, except for one other identical-looking house about two hundred yards away, which was empty.

The first time I saw the house, I looked at Max and exclaimed, "Are you kidding me?!"

"Isn't it great?" he beamed. It was clear that his idea of great and mine bore no relationship to each other whatsoever, a theme that would resonate for the rest of the trip. I was panting, exhausted from the long hike up the side of the mountain, and asked, already dreading the answer, "Where is the bathroom?" Naturally, it was the great outdoors. After the initial shock, and being mindful of not wanting to appear too whiny at this early stage of the trip and of our relationship, I decided to jump in and make the best of it, only because I knew the alternative was to be miserable. We had already rented and paid for the house for one month.

Almost every day, the melody and chorus of the Lemonhead's song "The Outdoor Type" went through my head. It was clear I was not as outdoorsy as I may have claimed from the comfort of my living room. In fact, I had never even been camping up to that point and couldn't light a barbeque without the help of a hair blow-dryer. I liked the idea of being the outdoor type, but that is where it stopped. Although I loved being in the mountains, I hated all the hard work it took just to survive. I hated having to dig a hole every time I needed a bathroom, and yet I loved waking up to the endless beauty that was constantly around me. There was electricity, sometimes, but you could never count on it. Nothing was easy. To have even a simple cup of tea meant we needed to start a fire. Bags of groceries needed to be hauled up from the village, cleaned, and cooked on the stove every day. It took hours to prepare food and clean up properly, so as not to attract unwelcome animal visitors at night, like bears and wolves; luckily we never did. Each day simply revolved around keeping warm enough and feeding ourselves.

It was both physically and mentally challenging, so much so that I totally forgot I had had cancer; I was too busy surviving! If someone had told me how hard India was going to be, I don't think I would have gone. In retrospect, I am glad I didn't know, because I never would have thought that I could have done it. But I did do it, with a lot of help from Max, and it was a good reminder that I *am* a survivor. It also showed me how protected I was from the realities of hard-core life.

There was no avoiding life in India. There was no TV to turn on and get away from it all, no bottle of red wine to open, and no place to shop—in the mountains, at least. I also realized what a spoiled brat I was and how much I took for granted. I started to face myself on that mountain, and I didn't like everything I saw. India became a mirror for everything about myself that was beautiful and repulsive.

After one month on the mountain, it was a relief to walk down to the village for the last time. I was excited to see the rest of India and hoped it would be a little easier. Max had carefully planned an itinerary full of sacred and special places that he had discovered on his travels, off the beaten tourist trail. Our plan was to slowly make our way toward Goa, a previous Portuguese province on the western coast, and stay there for the last two months, if I liked it. We stopped off in remote little towns and villages along the way, for days and sometimes weeks at a time, depending on how we felt, who we met, and sometimes depending on when the bus or train decided to come. Timetables and schedules were not taken very seriously in India.

I fell in love with the open-hearted Indian people. Everyone we passed in the villages would say "Namaste! Namaste!" It was the word for hello, goodbye, and thank you, and it meant "the light inside of me greets the light inside of you" or "the God in me sees the God in you." Imagine greeting people like that every day and meaning it—instead of "Hey, how's it going?" or "What's up?" and not even waiting for or wanting to hear a response. For me, "Namaste" felt authentic. There was a genuine friendliness that we encountered everywhere we went. They asked us all sorts of questions, with no visible trace of self-consciousness, which touched my heart in a way I never could have expected. "Where you from?" "You married?" "How many children?" "Sit down, I buy you a chai, you tell me all your troubles. Baba make them go away." Their brown eyes opened wide and gleaming, smiles beamed, and heads bobbed from side to side with excitement to make our acquaintance. It was hard to imagine having any troubles at all to tell these people who had, according to Western culture, nothing. They appeared to be happy with what little they did have, which made them rich in my eyes. There was an innocence and lack of sophistication about most of the people we met that was regal and beautiful to me.

We traveled through the country as cheaply as possible. Max wanted me to experience the "real" India. He insisted that we travel second or third class on all the trains, so we would be among the real people. That meant lining up for hours at a time to purchase tickets and scrambling onto the train carriages with hundreds of people to try and find seats close together. It also meant that we always had to chain and padlock our rucksacks to the legs of the train seats whenever we were taking a long journey, to ensure they would still be there when we arrived at our destination. The golden rule was: never part from your rucksack, passport, and money. That was the other reality of traveling in India. We always had to be alert and on our guard. You never knew who you were going to run into or what was going to happen. That is true everywhere, but in India, the extremes of every situation are in your face all the time to remind you, extremes of character, poverty, and beauty.

In a small town in Rajasthan, where we stayed for two weeks, we would rise every morning before dawn and walk to a Hindu temple across town. We were usually awake early, as the Muslim call to prayer blared through a loudspeaker from across the lake throughout most of the night. I loved visiting the ancient and beautiful temples and mosques that were scattered throughout the most remote places you could imagine.

The temple was situated on top of a steep hill that over-looked the entire valley. Large groups of people walked there every morning, like a pilgrimage, and climbed up the 108 steps to watch the sunrise. Everyone was panting and sweating by the time they got to the top. Hundreds of monkeys sat motionless, lining the stairway on either side. It looked as if they were forming a guard of honor. It was quite an eerie feeling to pass the monkeys' inquisitive stares each morning. As soon as the sun started rising from behind the mountain range, the temple keeper rang a bell that filled the vast desert surrounding us as far as the eye could see. A fire *puja* (ceremony) was then performed to honor the new day and the rising sun inside of everyone. Afterward, sweet *chai* (milky, spicy tea) and warm *chapatis* (flat, delicious bread) were served for breakfast. I loved everything about this ritual, except the journey to get there.

We had to walk through town in the dark, and the only light we had was from the small flashlight we shared. The streets were empty except for a few rats that would scurry past, a few street cleaners, and packs of skinny stray dogs looking for something to eat. As much as I disliked rats, the packs of dogs terrified me. I had never had a dog and was always a little wary of them. When I was a kid, I remember my mom always taking my hand to cross the street if a stray dog was approaching us, in case it had rabies, she said. I had never been bitten by a dog or ever had a bad experi-ence, but inside I was still afraid. Without fail, every morning, at least one or two dogs would go for me. Max would always jump in fearlessly, and they would back off. By the third morning, Max was getting tired of the same old scenario, and he didn't want to go through it for the rest of the trip. He told me the only reason they were going for me was because they felt my energy, which was fear, and it made them feel superior. If I could throw out my old story and tell myself a new one, he was sure my energy would shift, and the dogs would leave me alone. He was right. It took a few more mornings, but by the end of the week, I had convinced myself that I was not afraid of the dogs or the monkeys. Basically, I kept saying to myself over and over again, like a mantra: "I see the light in me, I am not afraid." "I see the light in me, I am not afraid." The light inside me became bigger than the fear, and I felt it too. It was quite amazing. The dogs must have seen and felt the light inside me too, because they backed off and didn't come near me again.

I was also amazed and humbled by the intensity of spiritual devotion that was omnipresent throughout India. In one temple we visited in central India, an entire family bundled in together, arms full of bowls of rice, sweets, and fruits to place on the altar. The temples were always full of women in colorful saris and Indian men and kids outfitted in jeans, with the names of American baseball teams emblazoned across their T-shirts. We were usually the only Westerners, and they welcomed us with opened arms. The atmosphere inside the temple was electric, with people drumming, clapping, and singing praises to God in words I didn't understand. It didn't matter, the emotion and the devotion were palpable. I remember seeing one grandmother lovingly push her young grandson toward the altar so he could place a flower on it and receive a blessing. Afterward, he went down on his knees and touched her feet, she pulled him up and hugged him close to her body, kissing the top of his head, and they embraced each other tenderly for several minutes. Seeing this immediately brought tears to my eyes. I didn't know why, but I was overcome with emotion. The people in the temple seemed to have connected to something that I didn't fully understand. I couldn't quite put my finger on it at the time, but it felt like it was a deep trust and confidence in a much bigger world, God, and universe than I had any comprehension of.

Four months after leaving the Himalayas, we finally arrived in Goa, which was a different scene compared to the rest of India. The province was spread across miles and miles of white, sandy beaches bordering the warm turquoise water of the Indian Ocean. Life on Goan beaches was unique, different from my other experiences in India. They were full of Europeans, Israelis, and only a few Americans. The people we met ranged from spiritual seekers to aging hippies to people looking for a good party. You could find it all in Goa. In fact, Goa felt like a break from India, which I needed badly. There were Italian and French restaurants that served coffee, wine, and beer, and they even had toilets! I was exhausted from traveling and desperately needed some rest. I also needed a break from Max. It was crystal clear to both of us that we did not have a future together, but we also had several more months of traveling, so we decided to stay together until we both got back to Ireland. All the things I initially loved about him were starting to drive me crazy, and I can safely say he would have said the same about me. It was a relief for both of us.

After four months of depending on Max for everything, from booking train tickets and accommodations to crossing city streets, it was good to arrive in a place where it felt a lot safer to go off by myself for a few hours. I rented a bike and would often cycle five miles into the small town, passing miles of rice fields and open space—I felt so free. It was amazing to feel the warm ocean breeze flow through my hair, which was almost down to my shoulders by then. I loved ordering a *masala dosa* (yummy curried vegetables wrapped in a light pancake) and a mango *lassi* (delicious yogurt-based drink) and eating them by myself at a little table on the side of the road. Goans were used to tourists, so no one usually bothered me. I would sit there for an hour or two, write in my journal, and anonymously watch the world go by. In India, I wasn't the girl who had cancer; I was just another white woman passing through. I loved roaming the colorful street markets and listening to all the dramatic bargaining. It always sounded like a fight could break out at any moment, but it usually ended up in bursts of infectious laughter echoing throughout the stalls. Then I would cycle back to the beach paradise, full of other white people, which seemed far removed from life on the street. As much as I enjoyed the beach, it felt strange to be living so separately from the local people.

Max and I had a routine we fell into after being there a couple of weeks. Every morning, before sunrise, we walked to a little cove at the end of the beach where a Dutch man in his fifties, who used to be a Buddhist monk, led a group of Europeans in a yoga practice for nearly two hours, consisting of 108 sun salutations. It was a struggle for me at first, but I stuck with it and ended up looking forward to it every day. Then at three o'clock, mostly the same group of people gathered on the beach for some kind of group healing sessions. When I asked what they were doing, I was told it was Reiki. I could hardly believe it. In Ireland, whenever I mentioned the word *Reiki*, people looked at me either blankly or suspiciously. Here, everyone seemed to know what it was. I was delighted. Anyone was welcome to join the circle, to give or receive, and all of it was for free. No one ever asked for any money; it wasn't about that. It was about people supporting people in whatever way they could. All different languages were spoken, but everyone in the circle seemed to be able to communicate by a gesture, a look, or a smile. No one ever asked me what I did for a living or how much money I made. These circles were always followed by an evening yoga practice to honor the setting sun.

Each day in Goa revolved around the sun and the moon. It was an entirely new experience for me. I always loved the sun, and was certainly aware that it didn't shine enough in Ireland, but I never paid much attention to where the moon was. In Goa, I noticed where the moon was and that it had a direct effect on our movements. I knew the moon governed the tides, from living in Skerries, but I never had a direct relationship with it before. The moon determined what times we could pass certain sections of the beach at low tide and reach the cove where the yoga and Reiki took place. The moon also lit up the sky and beach at night, and I found myself missing it for the three days it disappeared every month. There were all kinds of festivals throughout India too, honoring the new and full moon. It made me realize how interrelated and connected we all are—nothing is wholly separate or independent from anything else. This was a huge eye opener for me. So was the meditation retreat I signed up for.

During the six weeks we had spent in Goa, I often watched small groups of people walking in slow motion around some caves at the end of the beach and wondered what the heck was going on. I found out it was a *vipassana* meditation retreat that lasted for ten days at a time. *Vipassana* means "seeing things as they really are." It's one of the oldest forms of meditation in India. The goal is self-transformation through self-observation and introspection. All I seemed to be observing over the last several months was how much I was talking to myself! I decided I wanted to give it a go. Max had no interest in doing the retreat but encouraged me to do it. It was no secret he wanted a break from me too.

The retreat took place in and around one of the caves off the farthest end of the beach. The same Dutch man who held the yoga classes led it. He had been living in India for the past fifteen years and had dedicated his life to helping people see things as they really are. All he asked for in return was enough money to cover food expenses during the ten days, and people were welcome to leave a donation if they wished, but it wasn't required. The retreat was limited to ten people. For the entire ten days, we were instructed not to speak or make eye contact with anyone. If we had a problem, we were to go to him directly, no one else.

The women slept in hammocks provided in the cave, and the men set up camp just outside, on the beach. In addition to no talking and no eye contact, we were all asked to bring extreme mindfulness into all of our actions and movements. That meant walking in super-slow motion, to become conscious of every muscle that was involved in every action, how it moved, and how it felt—lifting your foot, suspending it through the air, and noticing the moment and the sensation when your foot touched the surface of the earth again. It looked strange to me when I saw previous retreat groups doing it, and it felt even stranger to be doing it myself. I was glad nobody knew me. The same went for eating. We had to bring mindfulness into lifting the fork or spoon, watching intently as we brought it from the bowl into our mouths. The same amount of mindfulness had to go into chewing and swallowing each mouthful. I was so hungry by the end of the first day, I had to use every ounce of restraint I had not to wolf down my rice and *dahl*. No one was even willing to make eye contact with me in sympathy.

As part of the retreat, we could partake in the morning and evening yoga classes in a normal way, meaning we didn't have to go super-slow—we just had to bring mindfulness into the practice. I so appreciated those classes! It felt good to be able to move beyond a snail's pace, and most importantly, I appreciated for the first time how my body could move and what my body could do. Before the retreat experience, I was usually busy comparing myself to what everyone else could do, and I was always measuring up short. By the middle of the week, I was able to be exactly where I was, without noticing or worrying where anyone else was. That was a huge relief. I became aware of how my body and breath were connected, in a way I never had.

The first few days, I seriously thought I would go out of my mind. It was exhausting to be mindful of every little thing. I was surprised by how much energy it took to go so slow and pay attention. I also became aware of how much energy I wasted by constantly thinking. There did not seem to be a moment when I wasn't having an opinion about something, either judging myself or someone else or making a plan to get out of there. I fantasized about what I would eat and do when it was over, and I spent hours making up stories about the other people on the retreat, just to keep myself entertained. I wondered what their lives were like, why they were there, and if the retreat was as hard for them as it was for me.

By the fourth day, something started to shift inside me. I wasn't sure what it was at first, but I felt less like running away. Then I slowly realized that I had stopped having so many thoughts; and instead of judging the thoughts I was having, I simply started to notice them. It was a huge difference, and I am not quite sure when it happened. I mostly noticed that my thoughts were not very important or very interesting. The thoughts must have gotten tired too, because they stopped coming so much, but only after I stopped paying so much attention to them. It felt as if the thoughts were screens or veils keeping me away from the reality and beauty of every precious moment. That is all they were doing: keeping me from experiencing the uniqueness of each fleeting moment. Around that time, I remember biting into a piece of watermelon and feeling an explosion of juice and sweetness in my mouth and crying, just because it was so damn delicious. Randomly, I would burst out crying at how beautiful everything was around me: the sky, the waves, the butterflies, the people—and I was not even stoned!

I thought I would never again be bored for a moment in my life. When I got glimpses of that beauty, I could hardly contain myself. My spirit felt like it was way too big to stay in my small body. It felt like I had just discovered the secret of the universe. I wanted to run across the beach jumping up and down for joy, shouting at the top of my lungs, shaking people, and screaming: "I am not thinking, I am not thinking, everything is infinite, beautiful, and love!" Then, in a flash, it would be over; I had started thinking about not thinking. Never mind, I knew I was onto something, and during each day, I seemed to sink a little deeper into each moment of the retreat.

Toward the end of the retreat, I was definitely in an altered state. I experienced feelings that I never had before. I can only describe them as overwhelming feelings of deep peace and love inside my heart. By the last day, all the thoughts, screens, and veils had fallen away, and everything I could feel and see was *love*. I realized that my thinking and planning in the past had prevented me from seeing this: the brilliant potential and love that was available to me in each precious moment. I remembered that scene in the temple months earlier, with the grandmother and the boy, and realized I was connected to them too and to the devotion, faith, and love they carried in their hearts.

It seemed that feeling would last forever, but it didn't. A few days later, I found myself getting annoyed at how laid back Max was and pissed off that the train back to New Delhi wasn't on time. Once again, I was trapped in my own little world, where my thoughts, opinions, and emotions ruled. But something had changed. I began to wonder if the altered state I had experienced at the retreat—when I felt consumed by so much love—was really my natural state. What if that love was always there, just longing for me to notice it? I began to believe that it was, but every time I tried to go back and recreate that same feeling, I couldn't. Maybe it was because it didn't exist behind me; there was no going backward to find it. It was within me, in each moment, waiting for me to step into it.

Before we left for the airport in New Delhi, I stood on the same street corner and watched a similar scene to the one six months earlier. This time, I didn't cup my hand over my mouth or clutch Max's shirt. I didn't see chaos. I saw a cow stop in the middle of the traffic and watched as rickshaw drivers swerved frantically to avoid hitting the cow and each other. I saw a smiling and toothless, hunched-over old man carefully roll a cigarette in the palm of his hand and give it to the young man next to him. I smelled heavily perfumed incense burning in the air that I imagined was a jasmine bush in full bloom, and my mouth watered at the scent of curry wafting from a vendor's single pot. I saw love.

The *vipassana* retreat was all about seeing things as they really are. For me, India was an initiation into understanding that things aren't always the way they really seem. I went to India wondering if I could find out who I was; India taught me who I wasn't. I wasn't just a young woman who had had cancer, who had left the corporate world, who was training to be a therapist, who was born in New York, who lived in Ireland, who was single. I wasn't just any of those words that I often used to describe myself. My experiences in India helped me to see life through a much wider lens. It taught me how precious and beautiful every moment of every ordinary day is, and I began to be even more grateful for my very ordinary life.

I discovered that I didn't need the same things, comforts, and possessions that I always thought I needed to complete me. It seemed absurd that the woman who, two years earlier, was running around Dublin in a suit and heels was the same woman digging a hole to go to the toilet. I was able to bear difficulties I never thought I could, and I found a light and strength inside of me that I didn't know was there before. I knew that light was an inner resource I could draw upon to face any situation in the future. I also realized that, just because someone else accepted me, it didn't mean that's all I had to accept.

When the taxi from Dublin airport arrived at my front door, Max and I got out, bowed to each other and said, "Namaste." We both meant it, and we both knew we would never see each other again.

CHAPTER

10

Walk On

Driving a car at night, you never see further than your headlights, but you can make the whole trip that way.

—E. L. DOCTOROW

U2 were coming to Slane Castle, and I was beside myself with excitement. They were my favorite band in the entire world (besides R.E.M.), and I could not wait to see them. Slane Castle is a fifteen-hundred-acre estate in the heart of Ireland, a natural amphitheater that can hold up to eighty thousand people on the castle lawn. It is a spectacular setting for a rock concert, and once a year, they open the grounds to host rock icons from all over the world. The last time I was at a concert at Slane Castle was 1985, and Bruce Springsteen was the main attraction. "Born in the USA," blasted across the Irish countryside, getting the attention of every sheep and peak-capped farmer within a five-mile radius.

Summer concerts in Ireland are a wildcard. When I first moved to Ireland, I was always amused by my friends referring to events and times in their lives according to the weather: "Yeah, that was 1974, when we had three great weeks in August" or "Remember that hot day in June of 1982?" Now I understand. There is a high price to pay for all the lush, green fields, and the price is rain, rain, and more rain. So when there is an outdoor concert, it either means a mud bath or one of the best days of your life. So I remembered that glorious, hot, sunny June day back in 1985 at Slane Castle as one of the highlights of my college years. The castle lawn was packed with eighty thousand fun-loving, beer-drinking, exuberant "Boss" fans that could hardly believe just how good life was. U2 would have to put on a spectacular concert to top that memory.

In 2001, my summer revolved around counting down therapy client hours and looking forward to seeing U2. The summer before, one week after I got back from my trip to India, the phone rang. It was the psychotherapy training institute, which I had left, offering me a place on the final year of the course. It turned out that the thing "that never happened," had happened. Someone dropped out in the group behind me, and I got their place. I would finish my training after all. To graduate, I needed to have a minimum of one hundred fifty documented and supervised client hours. That meant driving across Dublin several times a week to see my own clients, take part in my never-ending personal therapy sessions, and see a supervisor every two weeks, to monitor my own work with clients. Every time I spoke to a friend, the question always arose, "How many hours do you have left?" At times it felt like it would never be over.

The academic part of the course finished in May and so did the group therapy. As much as I had grown to love and respect each person in my new group, I was glad to be finished. I was tired and "processed" out; I felt I had delved deep enough into my past, my family, my fears, and my cancer. And if I heard the question "What was that like for you?" one more time, I thought I would scream! In spite of how jetlagged I was by my own therapy, I always looked forward to seeing my small number of clients. The dynamic quickly shifted once I changed hats and chairs. Despite the fact that I truly cared for my clients, I also felt burdened by them in a strange way. After all those years of training, I had the sinking feeling that I did not really want to spend my days working with individuals, talking about their problems. There had to be another way to help people shine and see how magnificent they really were, but I didn't know what it was. All of my colleagues had already started making plans for their private practices. I wasn't quite sure what was next for me, and that felt like a problem, especially since I had invested so much time and money into the hope that being a therapist would solve all of my career problems.

With each client hour that passed, the U2 concert was getting closer, and the national radio station infected the nation with U2 fever. It seemed like it was all anyone was talking about. The eighty thousand tickets had sold out within hours, months earlier. Luckily for me, my friend Siobhan's sixteen-year-old niece spent the night on the long line outside the HMV record store on Grafton Street in Dublin, to purchase the limit of four tickets, one of which was given to me.

One week before the concert, with only ten client hours to go, I received some frightfully disturbing news that extinguished all of my excitement and affected me far more than I could have imagined. One of my colleagues in the psychotherapy course had killed herself. Her name was Ann. She jumped off the top of an apartment building in a depressed and dreary part of Dublin. She was only thirty-three years old, a couple of years younger than I, and the youngest person in the course. Of everyone, I knew her the least. It didn't matter; her unexpected and tragic death shook me to my core. I was devastated. Her funeral was almost unbearable. The church was full of the sounds of bewildered and grief-stricken cries. There was a black river of people winding around the sacred building, flooding the surrounding Dublin streets. An entire community was mourning the loss of Ann. At the top of the church were her fiancé, parents, siblings, and large extended family. They were inconsolable. What happened? No one seemed to know or to have seen it coming. On the outside, she looked like a vivacious and sporty young woman, with her whole life ahead of her. But the inside was different. Maybe she never felt good enough? In any case, she wanted to disappear. Her sudden death scared me. In retrospect, I understand that her despair was not hers alone. We all felt it.

That tragic event awakened me to a level of sensitivity that made me realize something I already knew deep inside: I did not want to be the therapist on the other end of a suicide call. By then, I knew myself well enough to know that dealing with calls like that on a regular or even irregular basis would not be good for me or my health. Boundaries or not, I was a sensitive creature. It's not like I could vet every client beforehand by asking, "Do you think you are a likely candidate to ever contemplate suicide or serious self-harm? If yes, then I don't want to work with you." That's not how it worked, and I knew it.

A week later, I was still exhausted from the heavy feeling that had come over me with the news of Ann's death and told Siobhan that there was no way I was going to be able to go to the concert. "Wipe your tears away and come hear some music," Siobhan kindly and firmly ordered. Siobhan was my totally grounded friend, who had supported me throughout all three cancers, and who, not so secretly, thought that all the therapy, Reiki, and traveling were just a little too "out there" for my own good.

"Come on, you love U2, and we have been looking forward to this all summer. I didn't know Ann, but I know she would not want you to miss this. Besides, my niece stood outside all night for those tickets, so put on your rock-star jeans and get in the car!"

It turned out to be one of those memorable, absolutely fabulous weather days. The sun was beating down on fair Irish skin, new freckles were appearing every minute, beer was flowing, and everyone was high on life. Whatever troubles any of us had that day, there was no sign of them once the music started. By the time U2 came onto the stage, the crowd of adoring fans had been worked up into a cathartic frenzy. It didn't matter how fantastic the support bands were, we were there for U2. One red-headed, sunburned teenager, sitting on top of another guy's shoulders, summed it up perfectly when he roared above the crowd, "Feck Moby, we want U2!" I am not sure if Jesus would have gotten as much of a reception as Bono did when he finally walked out. We all went absolutely wild, screaming and roaring in anticipation for what was to come. I can still feel a rush of energy in my body when I think of it, and to this day, I have never experienced anything quite like it.

I jumped up and down, screamed, sweated, and sang along with everyone else, well into the night. Every cow for miles around must have heard Bono belt out, "Beautiful Day." I swear, all eighty thousand of us sang along as if we were singing for our lives. The sun had been down for hours when Bono announced it was the last song. It went over like, "Flights attendants, please take your seats," when the first bump of turbulence kicks in on a long fight. No one wanted the day to be over.

All the lights were turned down, it got strangely quiet, and out of the silence and darkness, from the screen behind the band flashed the words: "Leave it behind, Leave it behind, Leave It Behind, Leave It Behind, LEAVE IT BEHIND, LEAVE IT BEHIND, LEAVE IT BEHIND." I stood dumbfounded, staring at the words. They caught me off guard, and I let them pour into me. I felt as if God had opened up the sky and delivered me a personal message, in spite of the eighty thousand people who were also there. Then Bono started slowly singing "Walk On." Spontaneously the whole crowd started singing "Alleluia," over and over again. For me, it was one of the strongest and clearest spiritual awakenings I had ever experienced in my entire life, and it didn't happen in a temple or in a church or while I was meditating. It happened in the middle of a field, at a rock concert.

Tears streamed down my sunburned and freckled face. I knew it was time for me to walk on and into the next part of my life and leave behind the way I thought my life was supposed be. It was time to walk on and leave behind all the ideas I had constructed over my life about who I was and what I thought I had to do to be happy and successful. Leave behind the idea that I had to do something, just because I put a lot of time and energy into it, or because I thought I should, or because somebody told me I was good at it. Leave behind the concerned and disapproving looks of friends and family, who only wanted what was best for me. The only thing I couldn't leave behind was my heart and my intuition, which I had started to value, trust, and listen to more than ever. It was time to leave behind playing it safe.

In my heart, I knew I didn't want to continue working with private clients on a full-time basis. Although I had experienced the immense value of talk therapy, it was also clear to me that it had its limitations. It didn't save Ann. There was more to healing than talking. I could not ignore the feeling rising inside of me that wanted to deeply explore the healing arts and the power of the breath, the body, and the imagination. I had also experienced, first hand, the magic that happened when I let my soul be the pilot, instead of my head. I wanted to work with groups in a joyous and creative way. I didn't know what form or shape it would take, as it was more of a longing inside of me than anything I had ever experienced or could explain. It was time to leave behind the fear that I wouldn't be any good at it or that I wouldn't be able to find my way.

A few months earlier, I had seen an advertisement for a one-year, part-time course at Crawford College of Art and Design in

Cork, with the long-winded title of "Arts and Empowerment Facilitator Training for Groups." By the end of the concert, I knew I had to apply for a place on the course. I had no idea what it would be like or where it would lead me, but the very thought of it filled me with excitement, so I knew it was worth a shot.

A few weeks later, I graduated from the psychotherapy institute and got accepted to the course in Cork. I continued to see a number of therapy clients throughout Dublin, and every month I traveled up and down to Cork to attend the training. It was a totally different experience from the previous three years. It was challenging for me, in that most of the people on the course were professional artists from all over the country, who were already working with groups within their communities. It definitely tapped into my own insecurities around being not creative enough. I was so tired of the "not enough" syndrome; intellectually, I knew it was a waste of time and energy, but it had been ingrained for so long that it was hard to shake off. I struggled with it throughout most of the course, but I was determined not to let it stop me from attending and participating.

The course emphasis was on creating safety in a group environment so people would feel at ease enough to participate in the group activities. The goal was to boost self-confidence and self-esteem in individuals through activation of the creative process. For me, it was all about not having to know how something would turn out and still be willing to show up and have a go—just like in real life. It was playful and fun in a way I had never experienced, and it gave me the confidence to take more risks in creating the kind of life that I had only dreamed about: a life where my heart and soul led the way, no matter what.

I loved being around all the different types of artists on the course. Everyone brought their own unique energy and talents to the group. And they all helped me to see that I brought mine too, in spite of the story that was running in my head. I bought *The Artist's Way* by Julia Cameron and delved into the exercises in the book with great enthusiasm and passion. I wrote my morning pages religiously. Morning pages are three pages of unedited, stream-of-consciousness writing. There is no censor, no judge, no right way; you just let it rip onto the page, first thing in the morning, before your feet even hit the ground. You don't show them to anyone and you don't read them yourself—ever. You just write. They are guaranteed to change you and they do. I can't explain why.

For me, it was a great way of seeing how much negative self-talk I was still carrying around, despite the fact that I thought I wasn't. My inner critic and judge were sneaky and usually popped up just when I was on the edge of an exciting new possibility. Writing down my thoughts helped to get them out of my head and onto the blank page, where they held no power over me. I also wrote down a few positive affirmations that I worked with every day for six months. "I am willing to learn to let myself create." "I am willing to use my creative talents." And the scariest one of all, "I am an amazing facilitator and healer, and many people are coming to me." I would write them down, five times each, like writing lines in school, except it wasn't a punishment; it was a life-line. I was surrendering and releasing my old belief system to the blank pages every morning, and I was having more fun than I had in years. I even spontaneously wrote an *Artist's Prayer* one morning. It went like this:

> *O Great Creator, God, Divine Source, Light, Mother, Father, Universe, please help me to have faith and trust in my own creative process. Help me open my heart and let in self-forgiveness, self-compassion, self-love, light, and happiness. Help me to release my struggles, to surrender them to the Universe*

and relax into the world. Help me to stop seeking approval from others, so I can be my creative and authentic Self. Please help me believe in myself, so I can spread creative and healing energy around the planet. Thank you, Earth, for supporting me, and Universe, for believing in me. I believe in You.

At first I felt a little embarrassed by it, but I soon stuck it on my refrigerator door with a heart-shaped magnet, so I would see it every day. It inspired me to keep going. I kept up the yoga practice that I started in India, just because I always felt so good afterward, even though I was usually reluctant and lazy to do it beforehand. I never managed to do it before sunrise; it was more like before *Oprah*. I joined a local yoga class to keep the momentum going. The teacher's name was Olive. She was a very unassuming, low-key yet powerful woman and healer in her fifties, who was also a mother and a housewife. She taught yoga at the local community center and had a little prefab in her garden behind her house, where she gave Reiki sessions. She had been doing it quietly for many years.

As soon as we met, we recognized each other, even though we had never met before. I had been giving Reiki to myself ever since I had been sick, nearly five years ago by then, and had gone through a training and initiation so I could share Reiki with other people too, but I never did. I went for a Reiki session with Olive, and soon afterward she became my teacher and mentor. Later, she introduced me to a circle of other older, wise women, who ended up sharing their gifts and talents with me too. She encouraged me to practice giving Reiki to my friends and family and to rise above being afraid of what other people might think of me. Bingo! She nailed it for me. Although I loved "playing" at being an artist and therapist and believing in healing energy, I was afraid to come out to myself and to the people around me and stand up in it. I had been living in Ireland a long time, and the cynic and skeptic in me were alive and kicking. I thought people would laugh at me and think I had "lost the run of myself." Sometimes we need someone else to believe in us before we can truly believe in ourselves. Olive believed in me, and actually, so did most of my friends and family, even if it was totally different to how they were living. I was the one getting in my own way.

Sedona turned out to be my little healing house. I saved my money, bought a massage table, and started giving Reiki treatments to my friends. Word got out in the small town, and soon people started calling me and asking for sessions. I gave my first workshop in that little house too. As part of the course in Cork, we had to design and give a six-week workshop series, with real live people, and get feedback. I called mine "Creating Sacred Space." I invited three women I knew and asked them each to bring one person that I didn't know. I enticed them to come with no cost and the promise of tea and dessert afterward. It turned out to be an incredibly fun, healing, and empowering experience for everyone present, including me. I had no idea how sacred, beautiful, and life changing it would be for all of us.

During the six weeks, they shared secrets, collaged their wildest dreams, painted treasure maps, made altars, cried, laughed, drank tea, and ate a lot of carrot cake. They all left with a deeper awareness and appreciation of how sacred and beautiful they each were, and all of them continued on their own unique paths of healing. They were an amazing group of women, and I will never forget them. They trusted me, encouraged me, and inspired me to keep going. From that day on, I vowed to trust the Power that was guiding all of this. My heart and soul felt like they were on fire with joy. I knew that this was what I wanted to do, and most importantly, I felt that this was what I was here to do.

That summer, I continued to see a small number of therapy clients as well as Reiki clients, and I started designing workshops with different themes based around encouraging and empowering people to be their best, most creative, most authentic selves. It was everything that I had been working on in myself over the past five years, and I was the happiest I had ever been in my life.

But something was missing. I hadn't had much luck in meeting my Irish knight in shining armor. I felt happy and healthy and noticed men had started looking at me again, but it had been two years since Max, and nothing was stirring. There had been a few flirtatious encounters in the pub, always after a few drinks, but nothing to lose any sleep over. In fact, going to the pub no longer interested me and neither did drinking, which is what the whole social scene seemed to revolve around in Dublin those days.

As much as I loved my little healing house, my friends, family, and living near the beach, I started to feel constricted by living in a small Irish town. Everywhere I looked, women my age were pushing baby carriages. I knew that wasn't my path. It felt as if my spirit was longing to travel to a place where I could nurture and grow the ideas and seeds that were sprouting inside of me. I envisioned a wide-open, orange landscape full of unknown possibilities, a sky like a vast, blue ocean that never ended, and lots and lots of sunshine. I longed to express the creativity, joy, and unexplored possibilities that were rising up inside of me. I knew in my heart it would soon be time to leave Ireland behind.

I wasn't sure where to go. I loved the landscape in Sedona, Arizona, that I had visited a few years earlier, but I couldn't imagine living there full time. As much as I enjoyed my trip there, I felt it was just a little too New Agey, busy, and commercial for me. I started talking to a few close friends about how frustrated I was feeling inside and the need I felt to express the free spirit that was expanding inside me. I couldn't figure it out in my head, so I decided to throw it out to the Universe. I began mentioning my desire to find my true home in casual conversations, every chance I got. Soon afterward, my friend Beth-Ann from Los Angeles, whom I had met through the course in Cork, said, "Dude, you've got to check out northern New Mexico, sounds like what you are looking for." I had never heard of New Mexico before, and I didn't even realize it was a part of the United States! I did check it out, and she was right: it sounded exactly like what I was looking for.

A few months later, I landed at the Albuquerque airport. Little did I know that this place, halfway across the world from Ireland and vastly different in every way imaginable, would become my new home, and ultimately, change the course of my life.

CHAPTER

II

Dating, Amazon Style

Who we are looking for, is who is looking.

—St. Francis of Assisi

Dating—the word always elicits a reaction, which can range from giddy excitement to downright terror and dread, depending on where we are in life, how we feel about ourselves, and what kind of experiences we have had. What is this human craving to find a partner and be in relationship all about? As little girls, we are fed stories from *Cinderella* to *Snow White*, assuring us that the knight in shining armor will come and save us from our lot in life. We will live happily ever after, once we meet the man who truly sees our inner and outer beauty. Of course, we grow up and intellectually know these are fairytales, but the little girl inside never gives up hope. One day your prince will come, and *then* you will truly be happy. Princes come and princes go. What remains is the deep-rooted feeling of incompleteness.

To be incomplete is to suggest that something is lacking or missing. So without even realizing it, we set off on a search outside of ourselves to find that something or, rather, that special someone, to take the feeling of incompleteness away. That is how relationships unconsciously become unspoken business deals. "I'll do this for you, on the condition that you do that for me." Often someone feels they are not getting a good enough deal, and the relationship falls apart. The search continues. The problem lies not in the deal going bad but in the misunderstanding that the other person can complete us. We continually set ourselves up to be disappointed. We are looking for love in the wrong places.

If dating was complicated and confusing even before breast cancer, then the thought of dating during and after breast cancer was unbearable. I had just turned thirty-one and had not been in a relationship for four years. This wasn't by choice; I desperately wanted to meet Mr. Right. To make it even more complicated, I now had a secret to protect, which added a new and seemingly insurmountable obstacle to the mix: I only had one breast. I didn't mind sharing this information with other women in yoga classes or support groups, but I thought if I told men, they wouldn't see me as attractive or desirable. And I wanted them to. I was afraid they would compare me to a "normal" woman and would reject me. So, as a defense, I used reverse pop psychology—I rejected them first, before there was even a chance of any intimacy developing. I kept saying I longed for a partner, but my actions sent out different signals, and I found myself alone.

The common denominator in all my previous long-term relationships was that the guy always chose me. That meant the odds of being rejected were in my favor. I always went out with men who were underachievers and far less ambitious than I thought they should be. Somehow, that must have served its purpose in making me feel better about myself. By focusing on what they were not doing instead of on how I was feeling, it disguised the low self-esteem I held about myself. The men I dated also seemed to be full of self-confidence and happy with their lot in life, despite my secret disapproval of their lack of accomplishments. I was the one who was never satisfied and always thought there should be more.

I didn't want to settle and compromise. I also didn't want to look at why I felt so insecure when it came to dating.

I was a "serial monogamist." If I met a guy who liked me, I usually ended up going out with him for months or years until it was painfully clear that it was over. By then, it was usually too late to even pretend we would remain friends. The classic phrase, "It's not you, it's me" turned into "It's not me, it's you." When it was over for good, it was usually followed by a long dry spell of me wanting to be in a relationship and wondering if I would ever meet anyone again or ever have sex again. I would ask my friends: What's wrong with me? Why can't I meet anyone? And my friends always gave me the answers I wanted to hear: "You're great! They must be intimidated by you"; "The right guy is just around the corner"; and so on. That was all before I had breast cancer.

After breast cancer, I couldn't imagine who would want to choose me, with only one breast. Friends with two breasts always asked me, "If a guy had only one testicle would you care?" No, of course I would not care, but let's not compare lemons to melons, shall we? Okay, bad example, but you know what I mean. Women rarely view the testicles as an important feature of a man's attractiveness, and many women would be okay never seeing them. I am also a woman, not a man, and we think differently when it comes to, well, almost everything.

Every Saturday night, I would sit around the table with my other single, thirty-something girlfriends, and we would wonder why we still had not met that special someone. After we polished off an East Indian take-out meal and opened a second bottle of red wine, we would muse over the kind of partner we would like to have and fantasize about how wonderful and complete life would be when we found our soul mates. I am not quite sure where we expected to find them. We enjoyed each other's company so much that talking, eating, drinking, and laughing our heads off around one of our tables was certainly more appealing than going out and hoping we would meet someone. On Friday nights, my gay friend, Mark, came over, and we would watch *Sex and the City* episodes together, occasionally have a glass of champagne, eat dark chocolate (both for medicinal purposes, of course), and tell each other how fabulous we each were. It was much safer than venturing out into the singles scene in Dublin, which meant standing shoulder to shoulder in a crowded, smoky pub and shouting at the top of our lungs into the ear of the other person, just to be heard over the deafening music. As the night went on, it was impossible to hear anyone, as everyone got louder and drunker while trying to appear interesting and funny. The pub was usually followed by a club, where we would spend the rest of the night on the dance floor, pretending we didn't care if anyone came near us or not, yet discreetly looking around to see if anyone was noticing us. It was often brilliant fun, but by the next morning, it felt mildly depressing.

For years I was obsessed with the question, "When do you tell?" I would play out different scenarios with my friends, and each would offer suggestions as to how and when to break the news to an unsuspecting potential boyfriend. "Don't tell until you know they like you." "Straightaway, get it over with." "On the fourth date." "Maybe they won't notice." And my all-time favorite suggestion: pointing to my chest while saying, "This one is real and this one isn't."

That was the one I attempted to use on the infamous New Year's Eve of 2001. I say attempted, as I was too drunk by the end of the night to utter the words coherently. The evening started out harmlessly enough. I went to the local pub with a bunch of friends, where we rang in the New Year, and then we all went back to Mark's house to continue celebrating. I have never been

a huge fan of New Year's Eve parties. There was always so much
pressure to have a fantastic time (pretty much ensuring that you
wouldn't), and this one was no exception. After standing in the
kitchen for an hour or so sampling Mark's partner's new cocktail
recipes, I knew it was time to go when I started shouting, "I love
that song!" after every song that came on the stereo. Proud of
myself for noticing it was time to go, I thanked Mark and told
him I was leaving. Then Kevin walked in. Mark knew I had a
crush on Kevin, which sounds so juvenile for a woman in her
thirties, but that's what it felt like.

So, as any fabulous gay man friend would do, Mark pretended
I had just arrived and asked Kevin if he would bring me a drink.
Several hours, cocktails, and favorite songs later, Kevin walked me
home. I invited him in. We were no sooner in the door when he
gently pulled me close and started kissing me. It felt so good to
be in his arms, anyone's arms, so I closed my eyes and kissed him
back. Suddenly I felt his hands reach under my sweater and my
eyes flew open. Oh my God, I didn't tell him yet! In my mind,
I pictured myself calmly and clearly gesturing, while saying to
Kevin, "This one is real and this one isn't." That reverie was inter-
rupted by a loud thud; I knew what it was the moment I heard
it, but I couldn't bear to look. My prosthesis had hit the floor.

It was the first and only panic attack I have ever experienced
in my life. Without looking down, I immediately pulled away
from him and told him he had to leave that instant. He did. He
walked out the door without saying a word, and I sobered up in
a flash. I looked in the mirror. There was no trace of the goddess
who walked out my front door earlier that evening, and I cried
myself to sleep. The next day, I had the worst hangover of my life.
I went over every detail of the evening that I could remember,
but had absolutely no recollection of what Kevin's reaction was
the moment I heard the thud. Maybe he didn't notice? After all,

he must have been drunk too? I wanted to call him to find out, but I was too embarrassed. I convinced myself that I insulted him by asking him to leave and that he didn't know what had really happened.

Six months later, which was about how long it took for me to see the hilarity of the situation, I bumped into him outside the supermarket. I asked him. Turned out he did know, and he went on to say how badly he felt for not calling me the next day. I thought to myself, What a bastard. One good thing about only having one breast is that it sorts out the Kevins of the world pretty fast. It's possible that he was just embarrassed and too immature to reach out, but that never occurred to me then.

A couple of years later, there was my date with a guy I have come to refer to simply as the "ass man." I met him at a film festival in Santa Fe. He was charming, creative, and had a line for everyone; he was also very persistent in asking me out. I was reluctant to go out with him at first, as he was about a foot shorter than my five feet nine inches, and he stood directly eye level with my chest. I knew I was being shallow and eventually agreed to meet him after his third call. It had been a long time since I had been pursued like that—in fact I never had been—and I was flattered. I told him about my breast at the end of our first date. He responded straightaway by saying that he was "more of an ass man" himself and that my ass looked just fine to him. At the time, I decided he was an asshole for saying that and got a cab home. My male friends thought I was too harsh in my judgment of him, and now I think they were probably right. He was most likely trying to diffuse an awkward situation with humor, but at the time it fell flat, since I was hyper-sensitive around the subject. In his own warped way, he was probably trying to let me know that I was attractive and sexy to him. It's curious that my girlfriends and I didn't see that side of it then, and although I never went out with him again, it turns out he really was more of an " ass man" than the asshole I presumed him to be.

Living in Ireland, I had been exposed to all kinds of quick-witted and black humor. But now I was in America. My humor had definitely taken a hit. If there was ever a time I needed to see the funny side of things and to take myself less seriously, it was during this period.

I finally stopped asking for advice on, "When do you tell?" I realized there was no one answer or one-line-fits-all solution. Every situation and every guy was different. I had some positive, affirming experiences and some disappointing ones. On the positive side there was Steve, whom I told while clinging tightly to him for dear life from the back of his motorcycle. He pulled over, got off the bike, and looked at me with his eyes full of tears and simply said, "I am so glad you made it." In the end, we didn't make it, but it had absolutely nothing to do with my chest.

Then there was Paul, the broke writer who couldn't have cared less. He was so happy to be out on a date himself. Besides, he thought it made for a good story. Our story ended rather abruptly, though, as I got fed up picking up the tab every time we went out. I told him I couldn't afford to go out with him anymore. I am guessing he heard that a lot, and he didn't seem to mind.

On the negative side, there was Edward, the sexy filmmaker who made heart-wrenching documentaries on the plight of Native Americans. I was wildly infatuated with him for months. When we eventually had dinner together, I felt comfortable telling him. His films were so full of compassion, I assumed that meant he was too. I could see him tense up as soon as I told him, and he called me a cab ten minutes later. When I walked out the door, I knew he had completely lost interest in me. I was devastated and cried for days. Who knows what hearing the word "cancer" brought up for him? The word does something to people. I suppose he just couldn't cope. It could also be that he just wasn't that into me, but I have a suspicion that the word "mastectomy" definitely tipped the scales for him. That incident made me realize I would have to be ready for all kinds of reactions—I knew it had nothing to do with who I was as a person, but in the end, it hurt like hell just the same.

For the most part, the men I met were kind and didn't care as much as I thought they would. Yes, it was always a little uncomfortable at first, but we got over it. I cared more than anyone else did. I eventually figured out that most guys just wanted to meet someone that accepted them too, however they were. I realized that everyone has a hurt or a part of them that they think is damaged and that no one will ever be able to fully understand and accept. We are not alone in our insecurities; everyone has them. I think everyone has some secret they worry will keep them from being loved. So the question eventually shifted from "When do you tell?"—which put the emphasis on whether I would be accepted or not—to "Do I like this person enough to want to tell him?"

I was discovering that the more I accepted myself, the easier it was to be myself and tap into my intuition around potential partners. There was more to me than my missing breast. In fact, there were parts of me that I hadn't even discovered yet. Around that time, it dawned on me, like an "aha" *Oprah* moment: I had a choice. I could wait to be chosen by someone that came along and worry about telling him, or I could choose and name the qualities I wanted in a partner, put it out to the Universe, and see what happened. I could also choose to enter into a kinder and more loving relationship with myself and stop putting so much pressure on myself to meet a man. Playing it safe in my relationships was not keeping me safe; it was keeping me stuck, thinking I wasn't good enough. It occurred to me: if I didn't think I was good enough, was I also judging the men I met as not good enough? Maybe the harsh critic inside me was also serving as a barrier, keeping potential partners and intimacy at arm's length. It was time to start taking risks. I knew I would have to break my heart open even wider and have more compassion for the whole situation, including the men I was meeting. It wasn't only about my chest, it was more about my relationship to myself.

When I first moved to New Mexico, my new best friend Anna took me to a local Japanese spa where clothing was optional. I had never been to a place that did not require a bathing suit before, so it was a bit strange at first to see men and women of all ages and sizes sitting in and around a hot tub with all their bits hanging out, casually drinking green tea, and reading magazines. That was the "communal tub." Surprisingly, I felt uncomfortable because I was the only one there who actually wore a bathing suit. There was also a separate "women's tub," which I preferred. There was definitely a more relaxed vibe as women of every imaginable shape, size, and proportion lazed around the deck talking, laughing, and chilling out. It was especially inspiring to see how comfortable the older and larger women seemed to be in their bodies that were heading south fast, and yet they all looked beautiful and happy to me. After going there a couple of times, I told Anna how lucky she was that she could go whenever she felt like it and did not to have to worry if she had a bathing suit with her or not. "So can you!" she said. "You are the only one stopping yourself. No one else cares." She was right. I was the only one stopping myself. It sounded familiar.

The first time I went by myself, it was dark. I was naked, sitting on the edge of the hot tub, feeling very proud of myself for being so courageous, even if it was dark. "You must be an Amazon," a young woman with dreadlocks and tattoos said to me from across the tub. My defenses shot straight up.

"What do you mean?" I asked, in an unfriendly and suspicious voice. I assumed she was referring to the muscles in my arms, which I was self-conscious of at the time; I didn't see them as a beautiful then. I thought they were too big, and I was embarrassed. I had forgotten about my chest.

She looked at me as if I was crazy not to know what she meant. "Your scar." She placed her hands across her own chest. "Female warriors in the Amazon used to cut off their right breast so they would have a more powerful aim to shoot their arrows."

"Oh," I softened. "Well then, I guess I am a warrior." I had never heard that before, and I was grateful I asked her what she had meant. I have been going to that hot tub for over nine years now, and no one has ever batted an eyelid or asked me about my scar since. I carry myself differently. Now I know I am a warrior.

Shortly after that experience, I went for a hike with a friend who was not dating anyone either. Halfway into the hike, the conversation came around to whether or not we believed in waiting for one's soul mate. Both of us agreed that we had dated too many frogs and had waited long enough. Next time we dated, it had to be soul mate material; we weren't going to waste any more time. We decided to get clear and say what kind of man we each wanted to meet and declare it to the Universe. When we got to the top of the mountain, I threw my arms open, lifted my heart and my head to the sky, and declared that I wanted to meet a man who was passionate and spiritual and who could love me, see me, and "get" me. I wanted to meet my match.

Three days later, I met Vincent at a screening of the movie, appropriately called, *What the Bleep Do We Know*. It's a documentary film about interviews with prominent scientists and mystics, connecting spirituality and quantum physics. It makes the case that we have the potential to create our own reality by bringing consciousness into our thinking. Energy follows thought, and what you give energy to gets bigger and can manifest in the material world. Be careful what you think and wish for.

I noticed him as soon as I walked in, and I saw him notice me too. It was hard not to notice him; he was over six feet tall, had long dark hair tied back in a ponytail, and he exuded confidence. We talked and I thought he was sexy, successful, and attractive. When he called me a few days later, I knew he thought the same about me. He asked me if I would like to go windsurfing. Windsurfing, in New Mexico? Apparently there were a few lakes in the state, which I had never been to in the sixteen months I had been there, and the closest one was an hour away. I had never been windsurfing before, and I did not relish the idea of him seeing me in a bikini on our first date. Of course, that was the first and only thing I thought of, and yet I surprised myself as I heard the words coming out of my mouth and into the phone: "Sure, that sounds like fun!"

During the days leading up to the date, I daydreamed about all the potential disasters that could happen: my prosthesis falling to the bottom of the lake, never to be seen again; me clinging onto the side of the surfboard screaming for dear life—I wasn't exactly a water baby and didn't particularly like being in water measuring above my head; and finally, me undressing in public down to my bikini with a guy who could seriously break my heart. But then again, I had been alone for a long time, and I figured, what else would I be doing other than taking another risk? The worst thing that could happen would be that I was left feeling humiliated and embarrassed. I was alone anyway. It was worth the risk.

The windsurfing date turned out to be one of the coolest and strangest dates I had ever been on. He was ten years older and sort of goofy and nerdy, but in a sexy way. Mostly I thought he was kind. He was also clever in selecting this date activity, as he figured we would have an hour in the car to talk and check each other out, and then he could show off in the water. As soon as we got there, I told him straight out: I had breast cancer, I am fine now, and I have only one breast—the other one is a plastic stick-on, and I am worried it might fall out in the water. To my great surprise, his brown eyes welled up with tears, his face broke out into a soft smile and he told me I was both brave and beautiful. I took out the prosthesis, left it on the shore, and we had a blast splashing around in the water. The day of our first date was June 12, 2004, exactly seven years to the day of my mastectomy. I thought it was a sign. I always read too much into signs.

I ended up falling in love with him. Our relationship was a positive one overall, but we made one dire mistake. We got married. Finally, the moment I had waited for my whole life, since I was a little girl, had arrived. I was getting married, and I was willing to overlook the red flags, which fueled my reservations and doubts, to experience it. The marriage lasted only two years. We both projected so many ideas and expectations onto one another that we eventually drowned in them. I thought he was my knight in shining armor, and he thought I could take away all his heartache. Neither was true. Although we had been having difficulties, the final breakup and divorce seemed to come out of nowhere, and the ferocious speed at which it took place left me reeling. It was all over within three weeks. Divorce seldom brings out the best in people, and this one was no exception.

His way of coping was to try to move on as quickly as possible and erase all traces of me from his life. The house we shared was totally redecorated within forty-eight hours of my leaving; it looked as if I had never existed when I returned to gather my things. I knew then that all my hopes for an amicable ending were in vain. I did my last dance with him at his fast and furious pace, rather than fighting him to try and go slow. I was devastated.

I would randomly burst out crying in the most inappropriate public places. For some reason, it often happened while standing by myself on the ten-items-or-less express checkout line at Whole Foods. On other occasions, I could be laughing with a friend, enjoying sushi one minute, the next bawling uncontrollably into my miso soup. I remember going to see my dentist for a checkup and practically gagging on the suction tube inside my mouth when he casually asked me how I was doing. It was embarrassing for me as well as anyone who happened to be near me at the time. I didn't understand what was going on.

Several weeks after my marriage ended, I threw myself on Anna's kitchen floor and cried out, "This is worse than cancer!" I immediately wanted to take it back, but it was too late. Anna and her ten-year-old daughter had already heard me. More importantly, I had already heard me, and that is what made me pick myself up off her kitchen floor, dust myself down, and wonder what the hell was really going on. How could I even compare it to cancer? Then I realized some of the feelings were the same. It felt like my life was spinning out of my control, way too fast, as if the ground was breaking up beneath me, and I knew my life would never be the same again. I had no idea what was next.

I felt like I was having a nervous breakdown. After a few months, I realized it wasn't my nerves that were breaking down— it was the breaking down of a value and belief system that I had always thought was true. I wasn't only breaking up with my ex-husband, I was breaking up with my past. I never thought I would get divorced. No one in the history of my very Irish-Catholic family had ever gotten a divorce. But then again, I never thought I would have an abortion, be in a near-fatal car accident, or get cancer three times, either. I didn't know what to believe in or who to trust anymore. The divorce felt like the final straw in the shattering of a dream I had been carrying around for most of my life: to meet a partner and live happily ever after. It wasn't Vincent I was grieving, it was the end of the dream and the death of my old self. Like my ancestors before me, the Tuatha Dé Danann, it was time to burn my boats and watch all my old ideas of who I thought I was go up in smoke. They too had to let go of their rich ideas to be open to discover the mystery of what lay before them.

I thought my new beginning would start off all nice and pretty, but instead it was messy and ugly. Just like real births often are. Before getting married, I had spent a lot of time alone fantasizing about what the perfect relationship was supposed to look like. I realized I was dating according to those fantasies and ideals and not according to my own deepest needs and desires. All my ideas and beliefs around what it was to be married had been overturned. I had taken vows in front of my parents and my friends, and I had broken them. I felt totally disillusioned by the whole experience and started wondering what other deep-seated beliefs and values I was carrying around that I didn't believe anymore or had outgrown. I knew it was the start of the rest of my life. I just had to stop crying first.

In between the random outbursts of tears, feelings of anger started rising to the surface. I had kept what I thought was a dignified silence throughout all the divorce negotiations. In the culture I was brought up in, it was much more acceptable to be sad than angry. So I did not respond to the nasty and angry emails sent by my ex-husband, the ad he placed in the local paper in search of his soul mate, or the news that he had found and fallen in love with his new soul mate, only two weeks after the divorce papers were signed. But now I wanted to scream. I couldn't bear it. It felt as if there was a mountain of rage trapped inside me, lodged right behind my throat, and I knew I had to move it in order to move on. I thought of my experience in group therapy, ten years earlier, when I was able roar and shout my anger out, in the safety and presence of my fellow group members, and remembered how good it felt afterward. Looking around my small apartment, surrounded by unsuspecting neighbors on either side, I knew there was no way I could do that at home, without the police being called or my new neighbors thinking a crazy lady had moved in next door. I was desperate to get the rage and anger out of my body. I was afraid that if it festered inside of me any longer, I might get sick again. That is how toxic it felt. It had to come out.

One night in December, three months after the divorce, I phoned my friend, Jennifer, who had patiently been listening to me crying and going over the same details time and time again. This time, I told her that I was going to go crazy if I didn't deal with my anger. Her response was, "So deal with it. Why don't you get in your car, drive up the mountain, and shout your head off? You know how to do this." Initially, I laughed at the idea of putting on my long winter coat and boots over my pajamas, leaving my warm, cozy fire and couch, and driving thirty minutes by myself, in the dark and freezing cold, to the top of the Santa Fe ski basin. Then I thought, Yes, that's it—that is what I have to do. I *wanted* to scream my head off. Before I changed my mind, I quickly put on my coat and boots, grabbed my hat, scarf, and gloves, and headed out into the cold, dark night.

It was pitch black driving up the mountain, except for thousands of tiny, flickering stars, millions of miles away. I drove the whole way in silence, concentrating on my destination, imagining the stars would be my witnesses. Several times, I thought of turning back, half afraid of what I might find in the dark wilderness— and inside of me! But the trapped anger willed me onward. I was shocked by how black and still it was when I reached the top. I turned off my engine and kept my headlights on. When I got out of the jeep, I looked all around. There was not another car or soul in sight. I gave myself permission to begin. Straightaway the closed door to my throat flew open, and I cried out into the dark like a wounded and wild animal. I made sounds that I never heard a human make before. Then the words came. And there were plenty of words. They just kept coming, expletive after expletive; I was actually quite surprised that I knew so many. Some of them had been so appalling to me before that night that I had never even whispered them, let alone shouted them out from the top of a mountain. And I admit, it felt damn good.

Suddenly, I felt tired and had to stop. The moment I stopped, a light bulb went on inside me. I realized it wasn't about Vincent. No one could make me that angry, if there wasn't already something there. Sure, his behavior was a catalyst, but it didn't warrant (nor was it worthy of) the tremendous amount of anger that I was releasing. The anger coming out felt as old as the mountain peaks surrounding me.

Moments later, another wave arose, from somewhere deep inside me. "Never again! Never again! Never again! Never again!" The words echoed back to me from the darkness. I didn't know exactly what they meant—I didn't have a story about them—but I trusted them. I drove up the mountain the following two nights. I realized I was still holding on to so much anger and disappointment, for things not going the way I had wanted them to. The third night I stopped. My voice was nearly gone, and I was exhausted. It felt as if a mountain had shifted inside me. Somehow, connecting with the rage inside also connected me with the courage to move on.

For weeks afterward, I was on a high and was convinced that all the tears were gone too. I was wrong. More came later, but it was okay. They softened my heart, and I felt great compassion for my vulnerability and my humanness instead of feeling angry for crying about them. I realized my marriage had been a mistake. I was even relieved it was over. So why was I acting like a grief-stricken widow? Indeed, divorce was a kind of death, but it would not do to me what cancer could. I was here, and I was alive, and the possibilities were still endless. I decided to make some new vows to myself. The first few I made were: I vow to love, honor, cherish, and obey my own heart and soul. I vow to pay attention to red flags, even when I want to charge ahead and do it my own way. I vow to understand myself better and speak my truth. I vow not to hold on to my anger until it explodes. I vow to have an intimate relationship with life!

I promised myself the future would be different. I admitted there was a common denominator in all my dates and relationships—me. The fact was that dating before and after breast cancer still involved me, and my idea of me hadn't really changed all that much. A part of me still felt insecure, and it had nothing to do with my breasts. My previous relationships had all served as mirrors showing me something about myself that I wasn't able to look at on my own. It was time to look in the mirror again and start "dating" me. This had everything to do with how I saw myself, and less to do with how other people saw me. What if we took the time to really get to know ourselves intimately?

I had been doing a regular yoga and meditation practice for a few years, and it was a godsend during those first few months after the divorce. Each morning, I would wake up and head straight for my yoga mat. It was a wonderful way to get into my body and quiet my mind before I started thinking about what I would do next. Then I would sit for a while and watch my mind spin, until it eventually settled down and I could connect with that deep silence and light inside of me, which always made me feel like everything was going to be okay. There was a force far bigger than me at play, and despite feeling disillusioned by relationships, dreading the thoughts of dating again, and swearing off men, for a while at least, I prayed to keep my heart open.

Questions similar to the ones I had after the third cancer diagnosis started emerging. What is it all for anyway? What is my purpose? What makes my heart sing? What do I love? And finally, what brings me fully alive? I realized I had been looking for the answers in all the wrong places. I would never find them in another person or outside of myself. It was time to turn inward.

I booked a personal retreat high in the Sangre de Cristo mountains, about an hour's drive north of Santa Fe. It was quite literally in the middle of nowhere. There was a retreat house there specifically for people who were working on creative projects, and it was free, which was a bonus, as I was broke. All I had to do was email the owner and tell him I planned to work on my book and meditate. I would spend the week alone, meditating and writing. That was my intention. You wouldn't guess it from the bag I packed, though. I brought a half dozen books, a bottle of merlot, dark chocolate, and a few movies, just in case I got bored during the seven days I planned to spend entirely with myself. The owner informed me that the only other person on the property would be the caretaker, Mr. Heinz. We would share the kitchen, and I would have the entire upstairs of the house all to myself. It sounded great.

It was snowing when I pulled up to the gray stone house in my jeep. I was relieved to have found the place before too much snow had accumulated. The sun was just going down behind the mountain. I paused to watch it before turning off the ignition, so I could hear the end of the Rolling Stone's song, "Wild Horses," playing on the radio. The sky was a magnificent combination of purples, pinks, and oranges, and for a moment, I forgot where I was. Then I saw Mr. Heinz walking toward my jeep. He waved and smiled. As soon as I saw him, I sighed and said, "Oh no," out loud from behind the steering wheel. For some reason, I assumed Mr. Heinz was a decrepit old man, spending his last few years hibernating in the mountains. Not so. A tall man around my age, who looked a lot like Bono, was walking straight toward me.

Mr. Heinz helped me with my bags, which was embarrassing as I had way too much luggage for a one-week solitary retreat. We hit it off instantly, and before we even got into the house, we discovered we had both spent time in India. In fact, he told me he was just back after spending ten years there on his own spiritual quest. I stole a quick glance at his ring finger. I knew I was in trouble the moment I looked. It was empty.

I never planned to meet someone so soon. He never planned to meet anyone either. In fact, neither of us wanted to be in a relationship at that time. It just happened. It had nothing to do with my plans or me. I told him about the questions I was asking myself and my longing to know myself and God. Needless to say, I didn't get much writing done, but we did meditate together every day. I told him my life story and he told me his. We laughed, hiked in the snow, and had long, intense talks late into the night. I cried on his shoulder and he wiped away my tears. He told me of his adventures in India and his struggles upon returning to America. I made him tea and fed him dark chocolate. He cooked for me. We instantly became friends and, eventually, lovers.

His name is Mathew, and we have been living "happily ever after" since. Well, not exactly. We also disagree and often frustrate the hell out of each other. It is not a conventional relationship by any shape or description. We are very different people, with very different lifestyles. The difference in this relationship, from the beginning, is that we are both committed to finding and loving our big Self first and foremost, and that did not stop just because we met. In fact the relationship continues to challenge me to dive deeper into my own creative recovery every day, with a passion and enthusiasm to reveal even more of my heart and my soul to myself.

Divorce was a kind of initiation into a bigger life for me. It catapulted me into a deeper spiritual practice, one that centered on self-inquiry and surrender to Spirit. It involved the difficult and sometimes painful work of deconstructing my fantasies and learning how to love myself, exactly as I am.

The key to real intimacy lies in our relationship to ourselves. No "other" can ever complete us or make us feel worthy of love. Our worthiness comes from the very fact that we are born complete.

Mathew summed it up beautifully in a prayer—a love poem—that he wrote for me once, when I was struggling with some old self-esteem issues. I want to share it with you.

FROM YOU TO YOU

May the breath of God fill your heart

Release all past pains and hurt.

May you lay yourself down before the
* Light within You,*

Find your strength and peace there.

Know that you are the Love.

That you do not need to be loved,

Though you are loved very dearly.

I finally found True Love. It wasn't in Mathew, though; it was God inside of my heart all along.

"Who am I?" I believe that is the pivotal question in every creative recovery. I believe it's a question worth living for. I also believe it's a question worth going on a few weird dates for—it can break your heart open even wider and bring you closer to Self and Spirit, if you let it.

12

Land of Enchantment

No pessimist ever discovered the secret of the stars,
or sailed to an uncharted land, or opened a new
doorway for the human spirit.

—HELEN KELLER

All of my ancestors had a deep love and respect for the land. Both of my parents came from farming backgrounds, spending their youths picking potatoes and forking hay. I remember my cousin, Marie, telling me that when she was about seven years old, our grandfather, who always wore a tweed peak cap and had a pipe hanging out the side of his mouth, opened his arms wide and waved them to include all the green fields and the sky above and said, "God made all this." They were standing outside the thatched cottage where he was born, back in 1900, the same cottage where my mom and her eight siblings had also been born. Marie never forgot it. I am so grateful she told me.

The Irish poet and mystic John O'Donohue refers to the Celtic imagination as one that walks out the door and sees a "wild and alive landscape," and every living thing as vibrant and full of beauty and life, which also includes one's self and one another. In early Celtic times, the people did not worship God and Spirit enclosed behind walls. The entire landscape was sacred, and worship to the Divine knew no boundaries. When I was younger, I thought it was strange to hear my grandparents talk about the fields as if they were people. They gave the fields names and often referred to them with affection. In fact, it is said that the name *Ireland* is derived from the ancient goddess Eru and means "body of the goddess." The mountains were her breasts, the rivers her tears, and her divinity was made visible through the beauty of nature. It seemed that there was a much stronger connection between Native American and Celtic spirituality than I had ever imagined.

I had no choice moving to Ireland when I was a teenager. I wonder if that somehow hardened my heart to see what was beautiful about it then—and in turn, what was beautiful about me too. In contrast, the move to New Mexico was my choice, and the freedom I found softened my heart to see more and to accept more. I could more easily accept all of myself, and also accept that there were still parts of me that I did not yet know or fully understand. I realized my own soul was longing for a deeper connection to Spirit, and that unconscious longing must have been bigger than my fears of the unknown, or I never would have left Ireland by myself to seek it. The search led me further and further away from my comfort zone, until it eventually brought me home to a place inside my own heart that I never knew before. I found out that the more I embraced the world around me with awe and wonder, the more I was able to do the same with myself.

I'm not sure exactly when I first became intrigued with Native American culture. It could have had something to do with my second-grade teacher, Miss Moore. She was young and pretty, with bright red hair that fell down her back. She smiled, laughed a lot and wore nice clothes; she was nothing like the nuns who taught the other classes. I thought she was the most amazing teacher in the whole world. I knew she liked me too, since she often asked me to erase the blackboard, even though I was never the first one to put up my hand. During break times, with the popular and louder girls, I would scratch her back. It seems like such a strange honor, to scratch your teacher's back, but I took great pride in hearing her purr and say how good it felt, especially when I hit a spot that one of the other girls missed. She would always make a point of telling the girls who were there before me to move over and let me into her circle of admirers. She knew I was shy, and she always did her best to show me that I had a place there too. I quietly thought she liked me the best, and I loved her for that.

It was in Miss Moore's history class, while viewing a slide-show on Native American Indians, that I learned the name for a Navaho home is "hogan"—my last name. Miss Moore made a huge deal out of it, and even though I blushed and felt embar-rassed in front of my classmates, I thought it was the coolest thing ever. Later that year, when I heard about Pocahontas in history class, I was sure I was she in a former life, which was odd, as I had never heard of reincarnation before. But there was something about her character and her story that I loved and identified with. My mother insisted I was being ridiculous and told me to get it out of my head and not to tell my friends. I forgot all about it until we moved to Ireland many years later. The name of the place we moved to was Jamestown—the same town name as the place where Captain John Smith landed and met Pocahontas in the 1600s. This is a far-fetched and long-winded way of saying that, ever since I was seven years old, I have felt a strong and special connection to American Indians. I don't think I am Pocahontas anymore, but I still like the story.

According to Native American wisdom, we all come here with some special and unique gift to share with humanity. They call it our "medicine." They understand medicine as anything that connects you to the Creator and to all of life. It can be anything that gives you personal power and promotes the healing of body, soul, and spirit, not only for you but for all your relations. They believe we are all connected. So for me, the idea of moving to northern New Mexico when I was thirty-six years old was medicine for my body, soul, and spirit.

My mom and dad supported me when I told them about my plan to move halfway across the world to a place neither of us had ever heard of before. I told Mom it felt like the land was calling me—even though I had no job, limited funds, and no clue as to how it would all work—and somehow she understood. My mom sat beside me, held me, and said I could always come back if it didn't work out, no harm done. I was lucky I had been born in the United States, so I had both an American and a European Union passport, which at least meant I had a social security number and wouldn't run into some of the problems my Irish friends had encountered when they considered relocating. It eased my heart to know that I could move freely between the two countries. In fact, Mom hoped I would be back in a few months, after I got it out of my system; she figured I just needed a change of scenery for a while. She also said she thought I was nuts, and it was something she would never do. We laughed. We both knew it was something she did do. She set sail for New York when she was seventeen years old, and she had the time of her life. She didn't come back for twenty-five years.

When my sister Eileen heard I was planning to move to New Mexico without ever having been there, she offered to go on an exploratory road trip with me to check it out. It was a brave move. Historically, we could only spend a few hours together before red hair started flying. If you think you are on your way to being a conscious and light-filled human being, I suggest you spend a few hours with your family and see just how far you have progressed. It always keeps me humble. It's not that we didn't love each other to bits, we were just so used to rubbing each other the wrong way that it became the norm. We would say things to each other neither of us would ever dream of saying to a friend. We were close, in the way only two sisters less than two years apart can be close. Sometimes it's easy to forget that you are not fourteen anymore or that it's courteous to ask for permission before you wear each other's clothes, shoes, or underwear. Mutual friends and family were surprised to hear of our New Mexican adventure together, and we surprised them all by getting along famously. I think it had something to do with the magic of New Mexico.

I felt it the moment we arrived. The expansive, orangey-brown landscape, hugged by majestic snowcapped mountains in the distance, pulsated with beauty and possibilities. We walked out of the airport and into what looked like a movie set for an old cowboy movie. It was breathtaking. In all my travels, I had never seen a sky so clear, vast, and turquoise-blue; it seemed like it went on forever. It does. Unlike Ireland, the sun shined, all the time. It felt like it was up in the sky shining only for you. The land and the sky fed my soul in a way I did not know was possible. There is certainly magic in the Irish landscape too. It has an ancient, fairy feel to it that is equally powerful and soulful; but Ireland and New Mexico are polar extremes when it comes to everything else. For me, it truly felt like anything was possible. I was in love.

As soon as we arrived, I knew my intuition had been right all along. By the time I was on the plane heading back to Ireland, after our three-week trip was up, there was no doubt in my mind or my body: I was going to move to Santa Fe and make it my home.

As great as Eileen and I got along during the trip, neither of us flinched when the airline attendant in Albuquerque told us we would be seated separately, since we checked in quite late. It turned out that there was a spare seat next to each of us, in different sections of the plane, but neither of us said anything. Shortly after takeoff, a handsome gentleman around my dad's age asked if he could occupy the seat beside me. He joked that his wife, who was a few rows back, needed a break from him. They were on their way to Puerto Rico for Thanksgiving. I totally understood. We struck up a conversation and hit it off immediately. He was quite the talker and showed pictures of his sons and daughter, who were around my age. I told him I was going back to Ireland to sort out my house and clients and that I was moving to Santa Fe in a few months. He couldn't believe that I was going to leave Ireland and move to a place halfway across the world, where I knew no one, just because it felt right. When we got up to catch our connecting flights, going in opposite directions, he introduced me to his wife and gave me his business card. They both told me to call if I needed any advice on renting a place, because they owned some properties and knew the area well. Their names were Clarke and Judy. Eileen met them too. She told me to hang on to the card.

Four months later, when I arrived back in New Mexico, I called Clarke and Judy. Thank God they remembered me. They invited me to their home for lunch. While I was there, their daughter Anna dropped by. We hit it off right away and instantaneously became friends. After lunch, Clarke handed me the local newspaper, and by four o'clock, I was holding the keys to an adorable, fully furnished, one-bedroom apartment in beautiful downtown Santa Fe. It was a classic adobe with wood floors, thick mud walls, and huge tree trunk beams holding up the wooden ceiling. It looked like something out of those Southwest-style magazines, and the best part was the rent: only $650 dollars a month, unheard of in that part of town. It was a six-month sublet, and the person was rushing out of town quite unexpectedly that evening, something to do with a lucky break and a boyfriend. She was in such a hurry that she didn't have time to ask for bank statements, references, or proof of work, which was my lucky break, as I did not have any of them. It never occurred to me that I might need them to rent a place. There was no formal contract. She said I "had a good vibe," and we shook hands on it. Welcome to Santa Fe.

The central location meant I wouldn't need a car straight-away, which was good, as I was waiting for my mom to sell my pink Hyundai in Ireland before I could afford to buy a car. Don't ever buy a pink car if you think you may want to sell it in a hurry. It took three months to sell that car. In the meantime, I bought a secondhand ten-speed bicycle for forty dollars. A few days after I arrived, I walked across the street to a small, locally owned bookstore, and they hired me on the spot. I sold books three days a week for minimum wage. A few months later, when my mom eventually sold my pink car, I bought a secondhand silver pickup truck, a pair of cowboy boots, and a hat. I woke up happy every morning.

Anna, a former pottery artist, worked for the Santa Fe Film Festival at the time and seemed to know every writer, filmmaker, actor, artist, musician, therapist, and yoga teacher in town. That also meant she knew every waiter, waitress, coffee barista, gallery host-ess, and Whole Foods checkout person as well. The joke in Santa Fe, or "Fanta Se," as it is often affectionately referred to, is that everyone has either three houses or three jobs. I quickly learned it wasn't that far from the truth. If you wanted to live in Santa Fe and do what your soul longed to do, you had to get creative.

I had only been in Santa Fe a couple of months when I got a letter from Dublin saying that my insurance disability benefit from my old job was being cut off. It had been five years, and they figured it was long enough. I had trusted that it would last as long as I needed it, and it did. Yet it was still scary, stepping into financially unstable territory once again. Interestingly enough, my period returned a few weeks after the letter arrived. I hadn't had one for five years, as I was taking the drug tamoxifen to reduce my chances of another cancer recurrence. I had finished the five-year course of the drug just before I left Ireland, with no guarantee of my period ever returning again. When it did, I saw it as another sign from the Universe—at least I was in fertile, unstable territory. The day I left Ireland, a friend inscribed in a journal she gave me, "Leap and the net will open." I discovered that the net always appeared; in return, I had to be willing to jump.

While window-shopping a few days later, I was offered another part-time job, in a fancy dress shop downtown. It was only for a few weeks, to cover the busy tourist season. That is where I met Renee. She worked there part time, and this being Santa Fe, she also happened to be a Lakota medicine woman, who had bills to pay too. We had never met before but we recognized each other immediately. She called me "sister." It was the start of a sacred and beautiful friendship. Renee took me under her wing and introduced me to a road and a world that I had never been exposed to before. She taught me about the medicine wheel, invited me to sweat lodges and sacred ceremonies, and shared prayers, stories, rituals, and songs with me. All because she said she believed I was in New Mexico and on the planet to work with "the people," and I would need all the strength and the help I could get. The only thing she asked in return was that I receive and share the teachings with humility and a deep gratitude and respect for the Creator and Mother Earth. I thank God for the day I met her.

Walking part of the road with Renee opened me up to a whole new way of seeing nature and life. *Mitakuye Oyasin,* a Lakota phrase and prayer she taught me, means "all my relations." It invites us to see how we are all interconnected in the great web of life. The sacredness of each individual's spiritual path is honored, as well as the sacredness of all forms of life, our ancestors, and the life that will come after we have passed. I understood from a place deep inside me that we are indeed all related. It didn't matter what part of the world I was in—pain is pain, hurt is hurt, grief is grief, joy is joy, and love is love, no matter who or where you are. Engaging in American Indian traditions and practices awakened in me a deep appreciation for Mother Earth and opened me up, even more, to accepting and honoring all the diverse forms of spiritual expression around me. I realized there were many paths to God and to Spirit, no one better than another, and all were to be held as sacred.

Around that same time, I also developed an interest in Buddhism. I began sitting *zazen* with a group of people, a formal type of Zen meditation practice. We would also discuss the concept of "Buddha nature," our essential nature as conscious human beings, which Buddhists believe is alive and shining inside all of us, through the darkness, the pain, and the joy. One of the greatest things about studying Buddhism for me was being introduced to the deity, Kuan Yin. She is praised as a *bodhisattva*, which means she forgoes enlightenment and entry into nirvana, or heaven, until all beings have reached a state of enlightenment. She stays behind to help all of us and is widely known as the Chinese Goddess of Compassion. What I love most about Kuan Yin is that she is available to everyone; you don't even have to believe in her for her to help you. She brings compassion to the entire situation, especially where it is lacking most, including our own hurts, insecurities, and self-doubts.

Paradoxically, delving into Native American traditions and Buddhism brought me into a deeper connection with my own roots, awakening a Celtic spirituality, which was buried deep inside my heart and yet felt strangely connected to the landscape of New Mexico—also known as the Land of Enchantment. I had traveled halfway across the world, intending to leave Ireland behind, only to connect with it and my heritage in a more magical and intimate way than I had ever imagined was possible. The Land of Enchantment welcomed me home to Spirit and my true self with opened arms.

As part of my new life in Santa Fe, every Saturday morning I went to an African dance class, with about one hundred other people and nearly a dozen drummers. It was incredible. Dancing barefoot to the sound of the drums made me feel alive and connected to everyone in the room, even though I didn't know any of them. That soon changed. As time went by, I made wonderful friends, from all over the country and the world, that were also lured to Santa Fe by its magic and beauty. They were photographers, artists, writers, dancers, and dreamers. We all encouraged each other to follow our hearts and dance to the beat of our soul.

Socializing in Santa Fe entailed hiking in the mountains, dancing, taking a yoga class, or cooking together. It didn't revolve around drinking too much in a smoky pub, and I found that being clear to experience all of life was intoxicating. I had found my tribe. I felt free.

Santa Fe is a spiritual place, there is no doubt about it, and it draws seekers of every faith, belief, and religious orientation from all over the world. There are Hindu temples, pueblos, synagogues, and churches; there are Sikhs, Buddhists, stargazers, atheists, yogis, and every kind of energy and light worker you can imagine. For me, this was the place where I was able to integrate all the different aspects of my ancestry, travels, personality, and life. There certainly was room for all of me to emerge and integrate in New Mexico. Something else wanted to emerge too—a new name.

Ever since I can remember, I felt conflicted about my name or, rather, names: Margaret and Peggy. Don't get me wrong; I personally have nothing against either name by itself. In fact I liked them both, on their own, for different reasons. Margaret sounds quite regal to me, and Peggy sounds friendly. For years, I had struggled with having these two names, and I had different associations with each of them. By the time I got to Santa Fe, I felt like I had outgrown the identities I had associated with both names, and neither one felt like me anymore. The separateness between them no longer felt authentic. I wanted to choose a name that would integrate and represent all of me.

It was important to me that my name symbolize my passion for life and reflect more of the woman I was becoming. I had been discussing the idea of choosing and changing my name with some friends for quite some time, but I could never think of anything that sounded exactly right, and I also never thought I would actually be able to do it. Then one afternoon, while talking with a girlfriend, out of the blue I thought of "Pasha." Immediately it clicked with me, and I loved it. I had never heard the name before, but it sounded like "passion for life" to me. Literally in the next moment, my mom called from Ireland. I asked her what she thought, and she simply said, in her strong Irish accent, "Whatever you think yourself. Shur, didn't I change my name too?" I was surprised by her reaction and then remembered that she was referring to when she moved to New York at seventeen, and her well-meaning aunt told her that Bridget O'Hara sounded too Irish. Instead she should use her middle name, Josephine, which she did and is called by to this day. I saw it as a sign when Mom called, because I always see things as signs when I need encouragement and confidence, but I also realized it was no use seeking permission from the outside. I was the only one who had to give myself permission, and I was the only one who could make this decision. Of course, I was a little apprehensive and afraid of what people would think. My

Santa Fe world would be accommodating, but what about my friends in Ireland and the rest of my family? I knew a few people who thought it would be ridiculous and would most likely make fun of me and have a good laugh at my expense. But was I really going to let the fear of them laughing at me stop me? No, not this time. It was too important to me. Despite feeling nervous about it back then, I also was very clear that it was what I wanted to do. Besides, I understood that most people didn't really care about my name, and I figured the ones who did would soon get over it. It was my life and it felt right. So "Pasha" it became, and I have never looked back.

Later, I discovered that *pasha* is also a Persian title that means "leader," and in Gaelic, the actual word for "passion" is *paisean*, which sounds like "pasha" when it is pronounced. Without knowing it, I chose a first name that was connected to my Irishness yet released me from it at the same time, enabling me to connect with more of myself. Having the courage and the confidence to choose and legally change my own name was one of the most empowering things I had ever done. It has served as a symbolic initiation into the rest of my life.

When I moved to New Mexico, I wanted to leave the whole cancer experience behind me. I was tired of being "the girl who had cancer" and wanted to move on and into a bigger life than I had known in Dublin. Shortly before I arrived in Santa Fe, I had just passed the five year mark since the third diagnosis, which everyone told me was a big deal. I had finished tamoxifen and been given a clean bill of health by my doctors, whom I promised to visit every year. I did not have health insurance in the United States, nor could I have received coverage even if I could have afforded it, due to my cancer history. I decided it would be easier to get checked out every year in Ireland by the doctors who already knew me. This also meant I got to keep my new healthy life in New Mexico separate from the one that had revolved around cancer in Ireland. I believed this meant that I could leave everything to do with cancer back in Ireland too. Little did I know, the Universe had different plans for me.

I reveled in the freedom of my new life in Santa Fe. However, I still did not feel like I was fulfilling my purpose. While I was grateful for my part-time jobs, I longed to do the work that enticed me to move in the first place. I went to New Mexico in search of an open landscape full of possibilities and impossibilities, where I could expand both personally and professionally. My soul longed to express itself and to discover and pioneer new ways of living and working in the world. I had arrived in Santa Fe with only my Reiki table, one suitcase full of clothes, and notebooks filled with ideas for working with groups like the ones I had facilitated in Dublin. It was time for me to get the table and the notebooks out, listen, and get creative.

One day Renee asked me, "Did you come here for an adventure, or did you come here to work with the people, contribute your gifts, and make a difference on the planet?" Her question hit me like a bolt of lightning.

The Universe truly does work in miraculous and mysterious ways. Shortly afterward, I got hired to work in a nonprofit community art space called Hands On Community Art, a grassroots organization that offered a safe and friendly space for kids and adults to make art, for free—making art accessible to everyone. Initially, my intention was to offer some kind of women's creative empowerment groups, similar to the ones I had already done in Ireland. Their director had a different idea for me. During my interview, it came up that I had gotten interested in the whole area of healing through creative expression due to my personal experiences with breast cancer. It just so happened that one of their board members had recently undergone surgery and treatment for breast cancer and had discovered there was a lack of helpful and ongoing support after her medical treatment. Hands On decided they wanted to offer an alternative group to women dealing with cancer, which would be outside of a medical facility. They wanted it to be uplifting, focusing on life rather than illness. Their only problem was they needed to find the right person to lead the group. This was when I walked in the door—and they hired me on the spot

I loved the magical feel to the space, which looked more like a kindergarten playroom than a serious art studio. It was welcoming and non-intimidating; kids' crayon drawings covered the walls alongside paintings by skilled artists. I imagined how happy and proud they all must have been to see them on display. There were long white tables stained with paint spills and dozens of shelves filled with all types and colors of paint, crayons, pencils, clay, wood, magazines, paper, beads, and bits and pieces for use in collage or whatever else one's imagination dreamed up to create. Huge blank canvases, some of them broken, lay stacked against the walls. If they could talk, I imagined they would say, "Pick me up and see what can happen!" The broken canvases were the most interesting to me. I knew what it was like to feel broken. I also knew what it felt like to get a second and a third chance and to be able to connect with the beauty shining through the imperfections.

I thought about how intimidated I had always felt around art, especially before my powerful first experience of painting "All Hell Broke Loose," after my third diagnosis. Then I remembered how healing and empowering it had been to get out of my own way and get creative with the paint. It helped give me the confidence to get creative with my own life. As with lots of life-changing opportunities, I initially had some resistances. Since I knew how scary and intimidating art and cancer could be, I trusted I could hold people in that space, even though I still held some fears around not being creative enough myself. I did not go looking to work with people dealing with a cancer diagnosis. I thought the move to New Mexico was about leaving cancer behind me, not diving deeper into it. Little did I know then that the work was more about actively engaging with life than it was about the cancer. Life extended a beautiful invitation to me, in the form of supporting, facilitating, and working with groups of people who all had one thing in common. We all had heard the words, "I'm sorry. It's cancer." Luckily for me, I accepted that invitation. Life knows best after all.

At the beginning, I was as nervous as the women who showed up every week. Then we started talking and laughing. I realized how important it was for everyone to simply be able to say how they were, without rejecting any feeling or trying to convince anyone how great they looked. People could just show up and play with the materials on offer, without worrying about what it would look like or what it meant; although it wasn't just about creating art together. We breathed and dreamed together, shared stories and music with one another, and created a space that pulsated with color, possibilities, and life. An intimacy soon developed among the group participants, and it was beautiful to see how people blossomed once they felt they were being seen and heard for who they were, wherever they were. Sometimes women would come to just sit in the space and breathe in the creativity around them. They felt safe enough to just be and not have to do anything. I saw how taking creative risks, within a safe and supportive structure, empowered them to take risks in revealing more of their hearts and souls to themselves and each other. There was much more to everyone there than a cancer diagnosis. Being a compassionate witness for the women in the group made my heart sing.

I also realized that cancer is a part of who I am, and it's also a part of me being fully alive now too. It's a part of my life story, and maybe it's even the most beautiful part, as it invited me to journey deeper inside my heart and my soul to see what else needed to be healed. In October 2003, in the fertile, unstable territory of Santa Fe, my creative, spiritual "baby" was born. I named it Creative Recovery™. Its goal and mission is to transform a cancer diagnosis into an amazing opportunity to live your best and biggest life, with passion and authenticity.

My life, my story, and my experiences with cancer are my medicine to share with the world. We all have a story, and we all have medicine to share. Often we need encouragement and help in discovering what it is. I believe the journey of connecting with our medicine helps break our hearts open even wider, to discover the light and the beauty that is already inside us, longing for us to notice and to connect with something bigger.

My second-grade teacher Miss Moore showed me that there is always an opening in the circle. We just have to be willing to enter, no matter how frightened or shy we are.

CHAPTER

13

Creative Recovery

Another world is not only possible, she is on her way.
On a quiet day I can hear her breathing.

—Arundhati Roy

When I landed in St. Louis to catch the connecting flight to the small town in Illinois I had never heard of, I wondered why they asked me how much I weighed, when I was checking in. Of course, I rounded it down a few pounds and didn't think too much about it—until I saw the plane. It was a six-seater commuter, and my initial reaction was, "You've got to be kidding me." As much as I loved traveling, I was not a big fan of flying. The problem was that I was on my way to give my first keynote speech to a women's wellness conference and then a break-out workshop on stress management, called "Enough Already!" If there was ever a time I needed to practice what I preached, it was right now.

I stood on the stage with one thousand eyes looking at me, waiting to see and hear what I had to say. I could hardly believe it was happening. It was like a dream, except I knew I was awake. I could feel tiny beads of sweat gathering in my armpits and rolling down the insides of my new, pink wrap-around dress. All I needed was huge circles of sweat showing under my armpits for everyone to see. Just before I went on stage, I ran to the restroom, where my girlfriend, Anna, pulled out two panty-liners. "What are these for?" I asked her. "I am sweating, not bleeding!"

"Stick them under your armpits so the sweat doesn't ruin your dress," she replied, very matter of factly, "but first push the hand-dryer button and shove your armpit under it." Ten minutes later, I walked onto the stage with two panty-liners stuck to my armpits, wondering what had I gotten myself into. I looked out at the women in front of me, took a deep breath, and prayed silently to help get myself out of the way and let Spirit come through. Then I heard a voice, which I recognized as my own whisper: "You are good enough." I forgot all about the panty-liners and began to speak from my heart. It was a long way from the intimate circle of women at Hands On Community Art, where it all started eight years previously.

The weekly workshops at Hands On lasted for over a year before we lost funding, and seeing the effects it had on the women made me more determined than ever to continue the program and bring it to as many people as possible. I didn't know how that would happen, but I trusted that it would. I clearly remember every one of those courageous women who came to Creative Recovery that year. Some came every week for the entire year, and many long-lasting friendships developed. Even though everyone was very different, what was the same—a strong desire to live fully and passionately and, yes, cancer too— bonded everyone together.

One woman, Rulan, who was the same age as I, attended the very first group, and we have remained friends to this day. When Rulan arrived at Creative Recovery, she had no hair, and much of her flesh and muscles had been sacrificed to the brutal forces of chemotherapy, radiation, and surgery, all in exchange for the precious gift of life. Rulan had been a dancer since she was eleven years old and had performed with elite dance companies all over the world. Her life and identity had always been wrapped up in being a strong, powerful, and graceful performer. She carried herself like a brave warrior, but when I looked into her eyes, I recognized the sadness, grief, and confusion that lay deep within her; I had carried those feelings too. She told me that Creative Recovery was the first place she felt safe enough to surrender to her feelings, without worrying what anyone else would think, and she gave herself permission to feel what needed to be felt. Rulan was committed to moving through her grief and sadness and showed up every week. As the months passed, she discovered that the dance was still inside her, even if she didn't have the physical strength or energy to move like she used to. The dance of her spirit unfurled in the writing, collage, and art activities she participated in, surrounded by fellow survivors, who all served as compassionate witnesses for one another. During the year, she began to feel and see herself as a creator and found different ways to express her essence, truth, and understanding of life through the different projects we engaged in every week. This gave her the confidence to expand her creativity and incorporate it into her personal and professional life. She started making costumes and props, and lo and behold, found a new purpose in life: to become a choreographer and eventually the founder and director of her own dance company. Dancing Earth, now in its seventh year, is a nonprofit organization and the first primarily indigenous dance company in the country. In the past few years, she has done choreography for Hollywood films, working with Mel Gibson and Colin Farrell—a piece of cake compared to those first, uncertain steps she took in her own creative recovery.

Rulan invited everyone who attended Creative Recovery to Dancing Earth's first performance at the Lensic Theater in Santa Fe. It was a piece she choreographed in praise of life. We got dressed up, clapped, cried, and cheered her on; she was dancing for all of us. Everyone went, except Carol. Carol had passed away from stage four breast cancer a few months earlier. But not before she rode her Harley Davidson motorcycle to the group and offered to take each one of us for a ride.

During the year, the women witnessed each other's processes, pains, and triumphs as they talked, cried, laughed, and created. Mary shared singing. It was part of an exercise entitled, "Listening to Your Soul." First, I led the group on a guided meditation, encouraging them to trust the images that emerged, even if they didn't know what they meant. Mary saw the image of a caged bird and was inspired to create it with pipe cleaners and glitter. She had always been shy about singing in front of people, even though she had a beautiful voice and longed to be heard. The caged bird she created encouraged her to open the door and set her own voice free. When she was sharing her art piece with the group, she realized that the cage door was not locked; in fact, it never had been. When she discovered it was only her thinking that was keeping her trapped, she gave herself permission to sing and play. Tears streamed down all our faces as she belted out her version of Van Morrison's "Moon Dance" at the end of our session. She has been singing ever since.

Nancy finished the children's book she had started before she got cancer and illustrated it with the drawings she created during the year. She changed the storyline so that the book would help kids to cope when a parent had cancer.

Not everyone's cancer went away, but a new voice seemed to be springing up inside people. It was a gentler voice that whispered words of encouragement and hope, inspiring confidence and opening up new possibilities. Rulan described it beautifully when she said, "My soul's wounded cry became a softer song of gratitude for the daily ritual of co-creating with life."

I got excited about developing and creating a bigger framework for the Creative Recovery groups to take place in. My next stop was the Cancer Institute of New Mexico, where I decided to open it up to men and women at all stages of cancer. They liked the idea and hired me to create several six-week series and one-day workshops. I began to develop more themes and structured the workshops around healing a whole life, rather than focusing on dealing only with the cancer. What I heard in the groups and saw coming out in the artwork was a deep craving to be seen, heard, appreciated, and understood—not just as a cancer patient or survivor but as a whole person. I started changing the structure and asking people to introduce themselves by answering a series of fun questions that had nothing to do with cancer. I wanted to know: if they could hang out with a famous person for one day, who would it be, and why; what was beautiful to them; and what did they want to be when they were in kindergarten? There was so much more to everyone present than cancer. People realized that they could gain the strength and courage to face cancer by seeing how much bigger they were than it. That is what I did in my own way, without even realizing it at the time. Once people could make the invisible stirrings and longings of their hearts and souls visible by engaging in creative play, they could begin to have a relationship with parts of themselves they had not known before.

In one workshop, everyone made kites and decorated them to represent their connection to Spirit. When we went outside to the Cancer Institute's parking lot to fly them, Amanda's kite wouldn't fly. It was too heavy. She had covered it with so much glitter and glue that her kite couldn't take flight. Initially, she was disappointed, then she understood that she had been covering up her own spirit with all the ideas she had about who she thought she was supposed to be, which included how shiny and happy she thought she had to appear for everyone else, at the cost of her own inner happiness. Caroline's kite rode the waves of the wind and danced high above the Cancer Institute building. She told me later that the next time she came to the building for radiotherapy, she thought of her kite flying high in the sky, and she connected to Spirit while having her treatment, instead of to fear. It helped in transforming the rest of her treatments into more of a spiritual experience, rather than one she dreaded.

Working in this way challenged me to keep going deeper into my own spirituality and healing. The themes and workshops I developed grew from personal experiences and from being a compassionate witness to the stories and the artwork that people were sharing in the groups. It continues to be the most humbling, heartbreaking, and joyful work and play that I could ever imagine being lucky enough to be a part of. It has also helped me to recognize that I am still engaged in my own creative recovery, every day.

Part of my personal and professional creative recovery was expressed by designing new workshops every week, which was often challenging, but I loved it. The part I did not love so much was cycling or driving around town in my old pick-up truck, posting homemade flyers in every doctor's office and coffee house I could find, and wondering if people would show up or not. The hospital provided no budget for promotion—I was the marketing department. It was often frustrating when twelve people would sign up for a workshop and only a handful would show up. Don't get me wrong: it was always amazing to work with anyone who showed up, and the intimate group dynamic was powerful, but I knew it was only a matter of time before the program would be canceled if the numbers weren't up. Sure enough, after a year, the budget was cut and so was the program. What next? Once again, I didn't know.

All I knew was that my own budget was in diabolical shape. I had invested so much energy and time into getting Creative Recovery off the ground, not caring about making money, until the little bit I had was gone. I knew things were getting pretty serious when I was putting tampons and gas and on my credit card. I still had a small income from *Sedona*, my lovely little cottage in Ireland, which helped out paying the rent in Santa Fe, but it wasn't enough to cover anything else. Still, it was a comfort and it helped.

The Universe truly does work in mysterious ways. Soon after the program ended, my mom called to tell me that my long-term tenant was moving to Australia at the end of the month, and the cottage would be empty. Yikes! It was time to make a decision. In spite of all the struggles and uncertainties, I knew in my heart that I was on my soul's path in New Mexico. I phoned Sadie, the old Irish lady who had lived next door to *Sedona* for her entire life, and told her I was going to sell. When I left Dublin a few years earlier, she asked me to please let her know before I ever put it on the market. At that time, I thought I would never sell my little healing house. Knowing it was there for me to come back to made me feel safer. The next day, her grandnephew phoned me. We agreed on a price, and I flew to Dublin six weeks later to sign the papers. Now my boat was truly burned! But unlike the Tuatha Dé Danann, I took out the gold and silver first—I needed it to pay off my debts and get me started on another new beginning in New Mexico. Now there was no going back. It had to work.

Unfortunately, I was not going back to any work. I took comfort from a quote by Joseph Campbell, "If the path before you is clear, you're probably on someone else's." The path was certainly not clear. Just when it seemed like the group work I loved with cancer survivors was coming to a close, the phone rang. It was Christine, the photographer who took my naked photograph in New York.

Christine was actively involved in the Young Survival Coalition (YSC) back then, and she asked me if I would be interested in partnering with her to help develop and train volunteers in their Survivor Link program. I jumped at the chance. The aim of the program was to provide peer support for women under forty years old dealing with breast cancer. It connected women around the country and internationally. Our job was to train volunteers, who were all young breast cancer survivors, to be able to handle a phone call supporting another young breast cancer survivor. We wanted to ensure they were empowered with skills so they could listen empathetically, without fear or judgment, and learn to develop and establish healthy boundaries so they could continue taking care of themselves. Callers looking for help were matched with a young woman who had a similar profile, to help her deal with her specific needs. We both knew the issues facing young women dealing with cancer were most often different from older women. There was the whole gamut of relationships and dating, sex, fertility, pregnancy during and after cancer, careers, and what to do after the treatment is over, as well as the fear across the board of dealing with a recurrence or metastasized cancer. The goal of the program was to reduce the sense of isolation often felt and to make sure that no one had to face breast cancer alone. Christine and I combined our ideas and skills and designed a training program. We started traveling to YSC affiliates all over the country, meeting courageous young survivors who wanted to reach out and help their sisters. Survivor Link continues to thrive, and Christine and I have trained over two hundred volunteers to date. The generosity of spirit of the volunteers never ceases to amaze me. Their only obligation is to have one phone conversation with a specific caller, but more often than not, they end up developing friendships and sharing a lot more than their cancer experiences.

My interest and involvement in the YSC deepened, and over the years I have spoken and presented Creative Recovery workshops at their annual conferences in Washington, DC and Atlanta. The topics have included creative ways of managing stress, women's wellness, and making peace with our bodies. These were themes and subjects all close to my own heart and remaining breast! At one of my presentations, I projected my naked photographs onto a huge screen, to over one hundred young women and one embarrassed male sound technician. I did it to show them that no matter how we look, what we have been through, or how wounded we are, we can still enter into the sacred relationship of learning how to love and accept ourselves—exactly as we are. I understand what a daunting task that can be and also what an amazing opportunity it can be, to leave behind who you think you are supposed to be and accept who you really are. One woman emailed me afterward and told me she went home that night and undressed in front of her husband, and they made love for the first time since her mastectomy, six months previously. She was finally ready to see herself as the beautiful woman he kept telling her she was.

During the course of my own recovery, I discovered it wasn't only about making peace with my physical body. I believe I recovered and healed into a new life by making peace with my dream body too. To do that, I had to recognize and value the wisdom of the invisible aspects of my human experience, my creative energy and spirit, which included my intuition, imagination, hopes, dreams, and my non-rational brain. In an effort to bring people into a relationship with the wisdom held in their own dream body, I invited people to create body maps, as part of one of my workshops. I asked participants to lie on the floor, taking any shape they liked, while another participant traced their body onto a large piece of thick watercolor paper. Their body outline became the canvas for their body map. On the map they were invited to make visible their personal dreams, longings, and visions for themselves—no matter how outrageous, silly, impossible, or magnificent they thought they were—by depicting them on the human landscape they shaped with their physical body. They used paint, pictures, symbols, collage, or any combination of mediums they liked to express the invisible longings they held for themselves. Every body map told a story.

Rebecca had a particularly strong reaction when she stepped back and saw the map she had created. At the beginning, she was feeling quite small and scared, so she laid down in a fetal position to be traced. Then she started cutting out random images that she was drawn to from magazines, without knowing why, and placed them inside the outline of her small body. There wasn't enough room for all the images within the lines so she scattered the remaining ones onto the open space, outside the boundary created by her body. For some reason she couldn't explain at the time, she drew wings coming out of her back and painted them gold. When she stood back and saw what she had created, she could hardly contain her surprise and emotion. Most of the images she chose were beautiful nature shots of vast landscapes. There were open fields with wild flowers growing, long beaches that never ended, mountain ranges, and coming out of her forehead was a Sony 35-mm camera, with a long lens. Instead of only seeing her small and scared outline, she saw a woman full of natural beauty, longing to travel and explore new horizons, yearning to see her life through a wider lens. She hoped the wings on her back would give her the courage to fly above the small image she had of herself and take a leap into the life that was waiting for her. Rebecca also shared that the wings reminded her she was not alone and that she could call on her angels for help when she needed some extra encouragement to have a more adventurous relationship with life.

Over and over again, when people stepped back and saw their finished body maps, it gave them the confidence to enter into a new relationship with how they saw themselves, their bodies, and their dreams and to begin creating a new vision for the direction they wanted their life and the rest of their story to take. It is still incredible to see how alive and animated people become, once they make their dreams visible on their body map. Very often, new awareness of memories and feelings stored in the body are revealed, and these can then be inquired into, with the destination of healing in mind. It is also amazing to witness how people's initial discomfort with their body image can be transformed, once they are willing to see a different version of themselves that includes their creative spirit.

More invitations to present came from around the country, and I started developing longer programs and facilitating weekend retreats. The first one was in West Virginia. I will never forget it. I had been preparing for months and then, three days before the event, my marriage to Vincent broke up, and I was in the middle of a divorce. Non-negotiable life events often arise at the most inconvenient of times. I cried the entire four-hour plane ride. When the plane landed, I knew I had to pull myself together and put down my own grief and shock for a few days, to hold the space for the twenty women who were going through one of the toughest times in their own lives.

The retreat center was nestled in the foothills of the Blue Ridge Mountains, there was a stream flowing through the property, and large old oak trees and hiking trails seemed to branch off every few yards into the deep surrounding forest. It was magical. There was no Internet, cell phone access, or televisions on the property. The place felt so wholesome and pure, at any moment I expected to see Laura Ingalls, from *Little House on the Prairie*, skipping across a field. I was reminded of the poet Rilke's advice,

"During difficult times, we should endeavor to stay close to one simple thing in nature." Staying close to the beauty and the magic of the nature all around me helped to ground me in my own true nature and the purpose of my being there.

One of the poems I had chosen to work with over the weekend was, "Imagine a Woman in Love with Herself," by Patricia Lynn Reilly. Part of the exercise was for each woman to write a love letter to herself over the course of the weekend, place it in a self-addressed envelope, and seal it. I would mail it to them the following week. I encouraged each of them to write with abandon, knowing that no one but herself would ever read it. It could be an opportunity to enter into a new and loving relationship with herself, if she let it.

As a part of this process, I asked each woman to reflect on what it would look like to be a woman in love with herself. Some women had adverse reactions to the words being "in love with yourself," associating the phrase with being "full of yourself" or not being humble or kind or gracious. We explored where these feelings came from. Mostly they came from childhood—from well-intentioned, or not so well intentioned, comments from parents, teachers, aunts, or uncles who thought it was their duty to keep young girls small and sweet. The women sat in a circle for over an hour and talked about how many careless comments they had picked up over the years and had unconsciously turned into core beliefs. For most people, it was the first time they ever spoke openly in a group about it, and it was a great relief to discover that they didn't have to believe it anymore! Everyone was excited about taking some time for herself that night to write her letter.

Before we broke up for the evening, I laid out some Fairy Cards, just for fun, and invited each woman to pick one to help them connect the gentle wisdom of the nature fairies with their true nature. Susan, one of the participants, approached me in a terrible state. The card that turned up for her was *Beauty.* "Anything but that!" she wailed between sobs. The word *beauty* was so loaded for her and represented everything she thought she was not. She rejected the card and put it back in the deck. We spent some time together, and I asked her to tell me what beauty meant to her. What were the beliefs she held about beauty, and where did they come from? I then suggested she use the beauty of the nature all around us to hold those feelings for her and to ask herself some questions about them—maybe she didn't have to believe everything she thought?

The next morning, Susan approached me and asked if she could take back the *Beauty* card. There were only three cards remaining, and she was afraid it was gone. The card was there. *Beauty* remained and was waiting for her to reclaim it as her own. *Beauty* was passionately and patiently waiting for Susan to reveal her own beauty to herself. She did this by her courage and will-ingness to sit with what was most uncomfortable to her, which included writing a love letter to herself.

Susan wanted to share her letter with me; she wanted some-one to see it. I have changed her name so you can all see it. It went something like this:

> *Dearest Little Susan,*
>
> *I just want you to be loved like you love. Don't let others confuse you. Don't let the world, not noticing you, detour you from having the confidence to continue on your journey. You are unlike anyone, you are unique, and you are you! Continue to bless and be blessed. I will be there to hold you and to guide you.*
>
> > *With Love,*
> > *Big Susan*

I cried when I read it first, because it was exactly what I needed too in that moment. Life was calling to me yet again, in the form of Susan, to see the bigger picture, to surrender to a bigger power, and to trust. Love is the thing that strings us all together. It is our ability to be vulnerable, to love, and be loved that makes us human, fallible, and powerful beyond measure.

Later that night, I sat down and wrote a love letter to myself. Tears fell onto the page, but I kept going. On the final day of the retreat, Susan handed me her envelope to mail. I then handed her mine and asked her to mail it to me. She took it and gave me a book she had bought in the gift shop, titled "You Are Greater Than You Think." She wanted me to know that I reflected her greatness back to her. I never told her I was getting a divorce, I didn't want to take away from her experience, but I did tell her she mirrored back to me all that was worthy and loveable about myself.

We are all connected, so much more than we think. Those women, with their lovely southern accents, held me that weekend more than they will ever know. I read the book on the plane ride home, and I opened my letter a few days later. I have it taped to the top drawer of my desk, and I read it to remind myself of who I am, when I forget. Just like I invited all the women in the retreat to do. They invited me back to facilitate the retreat three years in a row. The following year, both Susan and I were in new relationships, with ourselves as well as with men who could see us.

The more groups I work with, the clearer it becomes to me that it is important to offer a wider variety of practical tools and practices that people can explore and bring into their daily lives. One of the practices that has helped me along the way is yoga. I had been going to classes for years and wanted to be able to offer yoga as part of my workshops. I decided to overcome my own old insecurities of wondering if I was fit enough and pursue the path of becoming a certified yoga teacher. I didn't just want to teach sequences and exercises. I wanted to make it a magical and spiritual experience that anyone could enter. More than anything, I wanted people to be able to have another avenue to connect with the peace and light inside of themselves.

Studying the origins and philosophy of yoga with a renowned yoga master from California, who also happened to be a dear friend's husband, gave me a much deeper understanding of what yoga is and how, when approached with humility and openness, it can help heal the body, spirit, and mind.

When I mention yoga in any group, the first thing I usually hear is, "I'm not flexible." I have now learned that there is so much more to yoga than being flexible. In fact, the body postures are only one part of a vast system of knowledge, which includes understanding that how we breathe, think, speak, and eat contributes to our experience of life. It is more about a lifestyle, one that encourages us to raise our awareness of all those things, as well as paying attention to the people we hang out with, how we feel around them, and the environment we live in. All of it affects our life experience, which sounds like a no-brainer, but most of the time, I think we go around wondering why we are feeling the way we do, without taking a look at how we are living. When I became serious about yoga, I also started looking more closely at how I was living my life and what I was "taking in" on a daily basis.

Slowly I introduced more organic food into my diet and loads of water. I cut down on caffeine and alcohol. I hardly drink any alcohol at all now; a far cry from my party-girl days in New York, London, and Dublin. Believe me, I could not have imagined that ten years ago, nor do I think anyone who knew me could have either!

I also know how intimidating it can be to step onto a yoga mat for the first time, especially after surgery and treatment, so when I teach, I make sure that everyone finds a place to enter. I tell people, "If you know how to breathe you can do yoga." It's true—you can do it standing up, sitting on a chair, or lying down. Practicing yoga has been an invaluable tool in the difficult and sometimes uncomfortable work of learning how to love myself.

After I had been certified as a teacher for a while, I brought yoga into some of my workshops and retreats for people dealing with cancer. Then I started teaching several classes a week at a residential trauma and recovery center in Santa Fe. The facility specializes in treating those suffering from all kinds of addiction, post-traumatic stress disorder, depression, grief, and loss. People travel from all over the country and the world for treatment and stay anywhere between thirty-five days to nine weeks, and longer in some cases. What I still love most about working there are the individuals I meet. They are people who want to heal, who woke up one day and realized they could not go on living the way they had been. I can certainly relate to that.

After I had been teaching yoga there for about a year, it was clear to me that the men and women that were showing up on the mat were not so different from the men and women I was seeing at my Creative Recovery programs. Creative Recovery wasn't just for people dealing with cancer; it was for anyone dealing with life. I met with management, and they decided to introduce it as a weekly adjunct, on a six-week trial to see what client response would be. They saw the results. Three years later, Creative Recovery is now part of the weekly program curriculum and is available to all clients.

As unique as each individual is, there is something that almost everybody I meet shares: a deep craving to be seen and appreciated and a deep-rooted belief that they are not good enough.

It doesn't matter what part of the country I travel to, where people come from, how rich, attractive, talented, or educated they are. Everyone I meet struggles with his or her own self-worth.

It isn't obvious at first. There are all types of disguises. Some people hide behind being loud and arrogant, others are quiet people-pleasers. Behaviors manifest in all kinds of different ways, as do the reasons for people seeking guidance. Usually, the different types of addictions that initially bring people to the center are piled on top of a previous abuse: emotional, physical, sexual—or any combination thereof. In many cases, individuals do not realize that. Instead of having compassion for themselves, they carry around a ton of guilt and shame, convinced that they are broken, damaged, and unlovable. It breaks my heart.

What I continually hear is that people are hungry for a connection to a higher power. Many feel that they have lost it along the way, and others yearn to feel it for the first time. For the majority, life feels empty without it. When I began researching and drawing from different spiritual traditions around the globe and sharing the stories, poetry, and myths that touched my heart, I realized, in the course of my own journey, that we are all in this together. We engage in earth-based rituals, explore the magic of the high desert, and use the medicine wheel and labyrinth on the property for ceremonies. There is a strong spiritual foundation, which is not based on any particular religious belief system, and that is why it reaches so many people. The invitation is simply life, where every breath is a second chance.

Life is something everyone has in common, as well as a deep craving to live it fully, as our unique and authentic self, connected to Spirit. It doesn't mean we have to know what that even looks like. The only requirement is a willingness to let go of the old ideas of what it is *supposed to* look like. That is the hardest part for almost all of us.

During the course of my journey through cancer and life, I have discovered that whenever I am feeling lost, if I let my heart and soul be the compass, instead of my plans and all the *supposed tos* that had been driving me, life gets better. This knowledge is the essence of my life, work, and play now. When we have the faith to know that we are never alone, when we have the will to keep going and the humility to surrender to Spirit and Grace when it comes, then there are no detours—only amazing possibilities.

For me and for the countless numbers of people I am honored to work with, looking back and letting go of the old versions we have of ourselves has to take place so we can move forward into the unknown territory of living beyond these small definitions of ourselves, to ultimately live into a new and fuller life. Initially, the process of letting go of who we think we are and how our lives are supposed to be is scary, and we often feel lost and confused along the way. At these times, the impulse is to rush back to the way things were, because it feels safer somehow, even if it is not totally satisfying.

Allow yourself to feel uncomfortable for a little while, and give yourself permission to rest in, and then navigate through, the uncertainty and the sadness. The uncertainty and the sadness are not the end of the story or the road. They are, I believe, a necessary part of the journey that we all have to get through as part of this shared human experience. Where there is life, there is hope—and joy and blue skies and thunder storms and sorrow and sunshine and sunflowers and friends and disappointments and rain and the smell of freshly baked bread and bad-hair days and dark chocolate and music and new shoes and on and on.

When I look back at my stories and my journey, I realize that my whole life was getting me ready to experience the life I am living now, a life that I truly love and am deeply grateful for. Being willing to take an honest look at our lives and our stories helps us to get to know ourselves better. It is especially important for us to get to know our old hurts and wounds so we can move toward healing them, instead of acting them out over and over again. We also get to know our attributes and strengths, which we can call upon whenever we need them, and we need them every day to keep going, to keep taking risks, and to keep living from our hearts. Then we can bless our whole life, even the parts we aren't so crazy about. Sometimes we need to "burn our boats" and "lose the run of ourselves" to find out who we truly are and to discover the life that is waiting for us.

Afterword

This is not the end. It can be the beginning of your creative recovery. The ancient Celtic triple spiral displayed throughout this book symbolizes that there is no end to the journey—life, death, and re-birth are cycles we flow in and out of continually. As you continue on your journey, keep this image with you as a symbol for power through transition and growth.

The following will introduce you to the forthcoming sequel, *Your Creative Recovery Workbook*, a practical guide and companion text to *Third Time Lucky*. This workbook will help you engage and actively participate in learning how to truly love your Self. You can find out more by visiting my website, www.pashahogan.com.

Please remember, there is no one in the world quite like you. You were born to shine out into the world, no matter who you are, what you are, where you are, or what you think. You are loved, loving, and loveable—no matter your history.

Until we meet again, may your journey continue to enrich your life, and may the road rise to meet you (an Irish blessing).

Getting Started
STEPPING INTO THE UNKNOWN

Just before I intend to start a new creative project, I begin to notice how much I need to do the dishes, vacuum, file my nails, redecorate the house, call my mother, catch up on all my e-mails, and plan dinner. Every time! It doesn't matter that I know this; I still do it. Everybody does. You are not alone in your procrastination. Why do we do this? I believe we put off these creative play times, work times, and fun times because we know, deep inside, that it will change us in some way. When we face a blank page, canvas, or closed book, we do not know what will rise up inside of ourselves, and most of us find that a little scary. The fear of nothing rising up to meet us scares us too—it may even be unconscious; it doesn't matter. Even though I now know how amazing and transformative it will be once I start, there is still a part of me that is afraid of what I might reveal to myself, or that what I produce might not be good enough.

Guess what? It won't ever be good enough as long as you believe you are not enough. As long as you believe you are not enough, no thing or no one will ever be enough either. All you need right now is to understand that the following exercises are not about the product. They are about the process, your process. They are about how you feel while you are doing them. And later, when you step back and look at the results for the very first time, it will be about the relationship you enter into with both the process and the result, and how you relate to them over time.

The next time you notice yourself booking a dentist appointment instead of gathering images for your collage, writing in your journal, or taking a long, hot bubble bath, stop and ask yourself, very kindly and very gently, "What is this?" Most likely, it is you putting off the very thing that you want most. So be gentle and be firm. It takes courage to start and it takes courage to change. This is your time to be seen and heard.

Be warned, your inner critic, judge, commentator will pop up and try to stop you. Letting go of perfectionism and getting more playful can begin by using these practices and creative exercises to help unleash that creative spirit of yours that is bursting to get out and be known to you!

The idea of playing has sometimes put the fear of God in me. Play? What's that? I don't have time to play. But remember, it is playing, not performing. Just loosen up all your ideas of how you think it's supposed to look, and see what happens.

Just for Today

Starting any new relationship can be daunting, especially one with ourselves. It's often temping to slip into habitual, negative self-talk, which, after all, only serves the purpose of keeping you stuck. "What if it doesn't work?" "What if I am no good?" "What if I am not creative?" Heads up, folks: almost every single person I have worked with has announced to me, off the bat, that they are not creative, including myself. So what if "just for today," you could suspend the negative self-talk and try something else instead?

A few years back, while struggling to write *Third Time Lucky*, I put together the "Just for Today" principles. They have become a guide for my day-to-day life. Since then, I have shared them with countless others, who have found them to be helpful companions on their journeys.

Noticing a habit, thought, or feeling doesn't always require us to analyze it, figure it out, or judge it. Whenever my inner critic intrudes, I use one, some, or all of these principles (depending on how loud the negative self-talk is) to keep me grounded in the moment and to help me remember it's only my critic talking—it's not me! The following "Just for Today" principles can accompany you on your journey too.

Just for Today . . .

☙

*I am breathing in warmth and kindness
toward myself*

☙

I am excessively gentle with myself

☙

I am greeting my reflection with a softened gaze

☙

*I am giving myself permission to make
beautiful mistakes*

☙

I am my own compassionate witness

☙

Prefacing each affirmation with "just for today" brings it right into the now, and that is where our power is. "Just for today" is manageable and possible; very often "always" and "forever" are not. I suggest you write them down on postcards and put them places you will see them, to remind yourself to silence the negative self-talk. My "Just for Today" cards have been taped to my bathroom mirror, desk, and refrigerator over the years, and there is one by my side as I write this now.

Let's have a closer look at them.

I am breathing in warmth and kindness toward myself. Right now, just stop and imagine your next breath is full of warmth and kindness toward yourself. Feel the warmth and kindness entering through your nose and immediately spreading across your chest, into your heart, and down into your belly, filling your whole body with tenderness toward yourself. Imagine that each breath is life rushing toward you, each breath a second chance.

I am excessively gentle with myself. Okay, I don't mean being kind of nice or not being too mean or hard on yourself. I mean being "excessively" gentle. Most people tell me they have no idea what being gentle with themselves looks like, let alone being excessively gentle. You can start by imagining how you would treat your five-year-old self. What does she need in this moment? A hug, smile, warm bubble bath, flowers, cup of coco? Something that lets her know you are here for her. Keep it simple and real. Enter where you are, without putting pressure on yourself. The excessive part can come by consciously tending to yourself with softness and kindness the moment you notice your harsh, critical voice creeping in. You can replace that negative habit of being mean to yourself with a gentler approach, and practice sustaining it each moment.

I am greeting my refection with a softened gaze. Usually we greet our refection in the mirror with a hard and critical eye. Our eyes scan the mirror each morning asking, "What's wrong with me today?" A new line, spot, gray hair? Next time, try softening your gaze. You may be surprised by the love and beauty that wants to shine back at you.

I am giving myself permission to make beautiful mistakes. People love this one! While attending a Zen meditation retreat many years ago, I spoke with the meditation teacher about my fear of moving forward in my writing and teaching. She asked me what was stopping me. My answer was, "I am afraid of making a mistake." She asked me to consider, what if everything we do is a mistake of sorts, and that it is our duty to make "the most beautiful mistake" we can in any situation, bringing the very best of ourselves to every decision? If you are willing to make the most beautiful mistake that you can, given all the knowledge you have at that moment, then it will lead you on to make the next most beautiful mistake and so on. This advice freed me up enormously. Making "beautiful mistakes," over and over, can free us from the obsession of being perfect and allow us to take the risks necessary to truly live life to the fullest.

I am my own compassionate witness. Often it's not so hard to have compassion for the person beside you, or for the person halfway across the world. But how about having some compassion for yourself? Not so easy sometimes; mostly because our first reaction is to chastise ourselves. Next time, the moment before you resort to knee-jerk, not-so-kind behavior toward yourself, try taking a breath (full of warmth and kindness), step back from the situation, and see if you can be your own most compassionate witness . . . just for today.

I encourage you to have a relationship with these principles and to make them your own. Carry them around with you, calling them to mind often. Some may speak to you more than others. Give them a try and see what happens. You are worth it.

Acknowledgments

If the only prayer you said in your whole life was
"thank you," that would suffice.

—MEISTER ECKHART

The idea for writing this book was conceived when I left Ireland for New Mexico, nearly ten years ago. I am deeply grateful to the team of beloved midwives who have graciously helped me deliver it into life.

I send my love and gratitude . . .

To Christine Benjamin and Melissa Pantel-Ku, fellow survivors and soul sisters, who nurtured me during the course of writing this book with your time, energy, and love, as we exchanged creative ideas, opinions, laughter, and tears. I couldn't have done it without you both.

To Jennifer Ferraro, for your friendship and professional advice and for reminding me when to push, breathe, relax—and rewrite.

To my readers of the first draft: Anna Darrah, Lucy Dolan, Gail Larsen, Eileen Hogan-Grant, Thea Witt, Betsy Millard, Lily Morrill, and Marie O'Hara. Your thoughtful comments and encouragement gave me strength and faith during this long labor.

To my team of editors: Stephanie Gunning, for your expertise, insight, humor, and help in educating me about the publishing process; Page Lambert, for your critical eye and loving heart in critiquing the manuscript and providing invaluable suggestions for making it stronger; and Mary Neighbour, chief midwife and copyeditor extraordinaire, who came in for the final push and delivery. A deep bow to you all.

To my *anam cara*, Mathew Heinz, for your love and wisdom and for holding up a golden mirror to me, helping me to discover, more deeply, what truly matters.

To my mom and my dad (who left his body shortly before I finished writing this) and my extended family, who are private people and not accustomed to appearing in the pages of a book. Thank you for your love, support, and understanding.

To Larry and Barbara Dossey, for your generosity of spirit, warm hearts, and support of this book and my work.

To Freda Hanley, for opening the door and being my first compassionate witness.

To my friends on both sides of the Atlantic, I won't name you individually, as I am sure to leave some out unintentionally. You all continue to enrich my life more than you know (even when we don't see or hear from each other often!).

To all of the teachers, students, and clients that I have been blessed to work with over the years. I have learned so much from every single one of you.

And most of all to Devi, for showing me the way inward and forward.

Namasthasyai, namasthasyai, namasthasyai namo namaha!

About the Author

A passionate believer in the integration of body, mind, and spirit for living a full and joyful life, Pasha has been designing and leading Creative Recovery™ workshops for over ten years. Her mission and greatest thrill is turning people on to the beauty and infinite light shining within their hearts. Through her healing work and creative exercises, she encourages people to stop believing everything they think they know about how life is supposed to go and instead start living from a place of wonder and curiosity, transforming fears into unknown possibilities. That is the journey she embarked upon at age thirty-one, when a third cancer diagnosis forced her to stop. She left behind the corporate world, trained as a psychotherapist, and began listening to the yearnings of her heart and soul.

When she isn't practicing and teaching yoga or Reiki, Pasha loves to immerse herself in the beauty of nature, hike in forests and mountains, travel to beaches, and breathe in desert sunsets.

A daughter of Ireland, she now lives and laughs in Santa Fe, New Mexico, and continues her world travels. If you would like Pasha to lead a workshop or retreat or speak at your conference, please contact her at www.pashahogan.com.

Further works by Pasha Hogan to help you on your journey

Intimate with Change: Meditation and Yoga Series

Change is the invitation life extends to us every day. Not knowing what that change will bring is often a source of stress and anxiety. Pasha's CD/DVD series helps you navigate change between yourself and the unknown, transforming unfamiliarity into a deep intimacy with life. Pasha accompanies you through change in a gentle and down-to-earth way that is accessible to everyone, even if you think meditation and yoga are "for other people."

Softening the Gaze

CD (70 min)

This CD offers two motivational talks and two meditations, inviting you into a kinder relationship with yourself and your inner critic. You learn to demystify your fears by getting to know and understand them, which enables you to take the next strides to a fuller life.

Yoga: New Beginnings

DVD (68 min)

Join experienced yoga teacher Pasha Hogan on a guided journey of self-discovery, self-acceptance, and self-love. Learn to allow your breath to lead your way—instead of your thoughts—by following her morning and evening yoga practices demonstrated on this DVD. Pasha's style of teaching is inspirational and non-intimidating. Instructions are given in a clear and gentle way, welcoming absolute beginners and experienced practitioners alike. This is yoga in service of *you*!

The Journey: No Detours

CD (73 min)

In this CD Pasha shares her personal experiences and insights as a three-time breast cancer survivor, inspiring you to lay down your burdens and follow your heart. It consists of three guided meditations, which you can use throughout your day. The *Morning Meditation* helps you start your day clear and centered, full of warmth and curiosity for new experiences. The *Journey Meditation* can be done at any time of day to help you lay down your burdens and relax more fully into life. The *Evening Meditation* assists you in moving into a restful and restorative sleep.

To find out more and to purchase *Intimate with Change*, please visit *www.pashahogan.com*.

CPSIA information can be obtained at www.ICGtesting.com
Printed in the USA
LVOW11s1725290616

494605LV00002B/427/P